IN CHRIST'S IMAGE TRAINING

LEVEL I
TRACK THREE

PRAYER

TAKEN FROM WRITINGS BY

PASTOR FRANCIS FRANGIPANE

PRAYER

Scriptures, unless otherwise noted, are taken from the *New American Standard Bible*
© Copyright 1960, 1962, 1963, 1968, 1971, 1972, 1973, 1975, 1977, 1995
by the Lockman Foundation. Used by permission.

In Christ's Image Training
125 Robins Square Ct
Robins, IA 52328
Phone: 1-319-395-7617
Fax: 1-319-395-7353
Web: www.ICITC.org

Published by
Arrow Publications Inc.
P.O. Box 10102
Cedar Rapids, IA 52410
Phone: 1-319-395-7833
Fax: 1-319-395-7353
Web: www.ArrowBookstore.com

CONTENTS

TRACK THREE: PRAYER

INTRODUCTION

Welcome, once again, to our time together. Our next focus will be to study and appropriate the intercessory prayer life of Jesus Christ. God's Word tells us that, amazingly, even while Jesus abides in glory at the Father's right hand, even as He receives unending praise from the redeemed, He still "lives to make intercession" for us (see Rom 8:34; Heb 7:25, 9:24). Intercession, rescue and redemption is the core nature of the Son of God. He is the "Lamb standing, as if slain" (Rev 5:6) at the throne of God. The more we are conformed to Christ's nature, the more we shall likewise intercede for others in the sinful world around us.

Intercession is more than prayer, but it always starts as prayer. Christ's crucifixion was an act of intercession; His prayer, "Father, forgive them," (Luke 23:34) was perfectly united with his sacrificial action. God will give us intercessory actions that are the consequence of our intercessory prayer life.

Before we embrace this course, let me mention something to our many students from other nations. When I speak of praying for America in these messages, please do not think I have exalted my homeland above your own. Read my prayer focus on America as an example of how you should pray for your country. Be assured that we pray for your people. Indeed, you should keep us informed of urgent national needs. Each of us should let our own nation be a primary focus of our prayers and prayer-inspired actions.

SESSION ONE:

NATIONS SHALL COME

TO OUR LIGHT

SESSION ONE AUDIO MESSAGES:

1a. Praying for America (part 1)
1b. Praying for America (part 2)

Chapter One

Ask of Me

We live in unparalleled times. Not since the first century have more Scriptures been fulfilled in a single generation. Each unfolding word brings down another mountain; it lifts another valley. In truth, the way is being prepared for our King's return into this world.

The Great Revolt

The Lord forewarned that, during the endtime, "many will go back and forth, and knowledge will increase" (Dan 12:4). Contrast our time with any other in history: Not only are we traveling farther and more frequently, but we do so in a world inundated with increasing knowledge. It has been our privilege to behold the prophetic return of Israel to its land (see Jer 16:14–15), and our misfortune to live when "the earth is . . . polluted by its inhabitants" (Isa 24:5).

As though Jesus were reading a news summary of recent years, His prophecies of two thousand years ago clearly describe our times. Thus, we are compelled to discern accurately the significant times in which we live. Indeed, of all the prophetic fulfillments of our day, one prophecy in particular rises with immediate implications. It concerns the "apostasy."

Paul warned, "Let no one in any way deceive you, for [the day of the Lord] will not come unless the apostasy comes first" (2 Thess 2:3).

The apostasy has traditionally been described as a time when many quietly slip into a "great falling away" from true faith in Christ. Depending upon your specific view, sometime before or after the apostasy the rapture of the church will occur. However, the concept of apostasy as merely "a falling away" is incomplete. The original Greek word for apostasy, *apostasia,* when used in classical Greek literature, meant "a political revolt." From this we understand that the end-time apostasy is not just a time of expanded moral compromise; it is a time of open defiance, warlike aggression, a political insurrection against the laws of God.

This interpretation of the apostasy is not an isolated view. The NIV, RSV, TEV, PHILLIPS, and NEB all render *apostasia* as "the rebellion." The LB interprets the *apostasy* as the "great rebellion," while the JB assigns a proper name: "The Great Revolt."

As we gaze in awe at the fulfillment of so many other prophecies, let us carefully observe: Mankind has entered an era of open revolt and outright rebellion—an apostasy—against the moral standards of God.

Today, we are witnessing a large-scale rebellion against godliness and moral values. Indeed, this brazen attitude has had a name for itself since the 1960s: the sexual revolution. And "revolution" is exactly what it is. Our moral standards have not only been challenged, they have been replaced by a non-standard, one which seeks to promote every sin from obscenity to homosexuality and witchcraft!

Those caught up in this mutiny against morality boldly defy the sway of God in our nation. They argue the only standard Americans have is the standard of individual freedom. In their view, freedom itself is the "god" ruling America, with self-indulgence sitting at freedom's right hand.

Yet, Jesus still wants this nation. Though the apostasy will certainly intensify, we must remember it is only one of many prophecies unfolding in our day. The same Divine Word which warned of the Great Rebellion also purposed that God's kingdom shall crush and put an end to all nations (see Dan 2:44).

Yes, evil shall mature into full rebellion, but good is also ripening into full Christlikeness! (see Matt 13:40–43; John 17:22–23) Yes, the apostasy shall reveal the nature of Satan, but the true church shall manifest the nature of Christ! Jesus is not only coming in the skies, He is coming "to be glorified in His saints on that day, and to be marveled at among all who have believed" (2 Thess 1:10). What seems to be Satan's hour, full of darkness and rebellion, is simply the opportunity for grace to abound to the glory of God in the church!

SEATED WITH CHRIST!

The Second Psalm, perhaps more then any other Bible text, accurately portrays the spirit of our time. Indeed, it also proclaims our correct response to Satan's bold advance. Although it was quoted by the early church (see Acts 4:25–26), God has set its full realization for the end of this age.

"Why are the nations in an uproar, and the peoples devising a vain thing? The kings of the earth take their stand and the rulers take counsel together against the Lord and against His Anointed, saying, 'Let us tear their fetters apart, and cast away their cords from us!' " (Ps 2:1–3)

Although "the rebellion" reveals itself worldwide in many ways, in America many of our leaders have certainly been counseling together "against the Lord" in their recent decisions. We see it in the legal protection offered the gay movement and the shelter provided for satanic rock music. Again, our anti-censorship laws, like armor plating, take their stand against the Lord, shielding the perversity of our entertainment industry. The cry of those in rebellion hammers relentlessly upon the fetters of moral restraint!

This railing against God has not gone unnoticed in heaven. Is the Almighty confounded? Has fear concerning recent developments gripped the Lord's heart? No. The Psalm continues, "He who sits in the heavens laughs, the Lord scoffs at them. Then He will speak to them in His anger and terrify them in His fury" (Ps 2:4–5).

The Lord laughs at the foolishness of those in the rebellion, that they imagine God's judgments cannot reach them. Why then, you ask, does the Lord delay His full judgment? The Lord waits for us, His church. For while the world shall demand, and receive, the reign of hell, the goal of the praying church shall be for the reign of heaven. You see, all of God's prophecies shall be fulfilled: those concerning evil and those concerning good. The Lord has purposed to have a "bride without spot or wrinkle" and a "kingdom" of wheat without tares. The transformation of the church will be fulfilled as surely as the increase of knowledge, the return of Israel and the apostasy itself.

Thus, with great fear and holy trembling, we must review what God has promised concerning us! Let us remember, the Lord is not alone in the heavens. According to His Word, He has seated us with Him in the heavenly places (see Eph 2:6). It is time for our identity as Christians to shift. Our nationalities only define our ambassador status; our true citizenship is in heaven (see Phil 3:20). And if God is laughing at the mocking of those in the rebellion, let us also, as His subjects, share His confidence!

Thus, He commands us to sit with Him in the completeness of His purpose. He requires us not only to live without fear but to stand in prayer for these very nations which defy Him! Listen again to this Second Psalm, for in the very context of worldwide rebellion against Him, it records the most remarkable discourse.

"Ask of Me," the Father says to the Son, "and I will surely give the nations as Your inheritance, and the very ends of the earth as Your possession" (Ps 2:8). This request has little to do with the goodness of the church, but everything to do with the virtue of Christ and the love of the Father toward Him. Look around you: When I first came to Christ in 1970, churches in America were deeply divided and rather cold in organized prayer. Today, leaders of denominations are working together, and over a quarter of a million American churches are moving toward deeper unity and increased prayer for this nation. Jesus has asked the Father for the United States, and in response the prayer movement has been born!

As Christ's church, we do not deserve a national revival, but Jesus does! As His representatives, in His name and virtue, we ask of the Father for this nation! More than an expression of faith, our prayer is actually an act of obedience: We are commanded to ask God for the nations!

Therefore, while the perverse strive toward complete rejection of God, even as their mocking words fill the air with curses, God's unchangeable promise to His Son, and to His church as Christ's body, is *"Ask of Me, and I will surely give the nations!"* As violence, New Age religions and witchcraft flourish in our schools, *ask* God for this nation. While all restraint is removed from the entertainment industry, *ask* God for this nation! While perversity dresses in normalcy, *ask* God for America! While abortion, partial birth abortion and the abortion pill remain protected by laws, *ask* God with confidence, with boldness, with faith for our land.

He who sits in the heavens, laughs. So, put away discouragement; repent of fretting. The more we accept our place in the divine plan, the more we shall laugh at the enemies' plans. The faith that relentlessly asks God, pleases God. Now, as the fullness of the times unfolds, as the world around us clothes itself in prophetic fulfillments, let us put away unbelief; let us repent for withdrawal. For it is a time to boldly ask of God. He has promised, He will give the nations as an inheritance to Christ!

Let's pray: *Lord Jesus, how blessed we are that as evil matures into full rebellion, Your church matures into full Christlikeness. Teach me to pray for my inheritance, my nation. Use me to stand in the gap until my people become Your people.*

—FROM THE *ICIT* WEEKLY MAILER

SELF TEST, CHAPTER ONE

Remember, we are looking for answers that correspond with this training. Please write out your essay answers, allowing the Holy Spirit to provoke your thoughts. You may want to use them for group discussion. Note: we do not provide answers to essay questions. To check your multiple choice answers, see answer key in the next session.

Chapter 1, Essay #1: In what ways do you see that your true citizenship is in heaven?

Chapter 1, Essay #2: Explain why we shouldn't fear accepting our place in the divine plan?

1. In addition to a "falling away from the faith," how have many Bible translations defined the end-time apostasy?
    a. It is a time of open defiance, warlike aggression, a political insurrection against the laws of God.
    b. It is a time when churches allow dancing.
    c. It is a time of peacefulness.
    d. both b & c

2. Today we are witnessing apostasy in what way?
   a. large scale rebellion against godliness and moral values.
   b. a nation greatly challenged to higher moral standards.
   c. moral standards replaced by a non-standard.
   d. both a & c

3. Scripture reveals (Matt 13:40–43, John 17:22–23) that while evil shall mature into full rebellion, so good will _____.
   a. fade away
   b. ripen into full Christlikeness
   c. take over works
   d. be overcome by darkness

4. How does God respond to the apostasy and Satan's advance, as Psalm 2 states, "railing against God"?
   a. He laughs and scoffs at the foolishness of those in rebellion.
   b. He is confounded.
   c. He waits for us, His church, to be transformed.
   d. both a & c

5. The Lord has purposed to have a _____ and a _____ without tares.
   a. time of judgment, church
   b. peaceful world, heaven
   c. bride without spot or wrinkle, kingdom of wheat
   d. both a & b

6. As all of the Lord's prophecies shall be fulfilled, what does this include?
   a. transformation of the church, worldwide harvest, increase of knowledge
   b. the return of Israel, apostasy
   c. world peace
   d. both a & b

7. In response to apostasy, we are commanded to:
   a. be seated with Christ in the completeness of His purpose.
   b. demand righteousness of the world around us.
   c. live without fear, pray for the very nations which defy Him.
   d. both a & c

8. If we will "ask of God" (Ps 2), He has promised _____.
   a. material items
   b. He will give the nations as an inheritance
   c. nothing
   d. increased faith

> **QUOTE:**
>
> *"[God] commands us to sit with Him in the completeness of His purpose. He requires us not only to live without fear but to stand in prayer for these very nations which defy Him! . . . 'Ask of Me,' the Father says to the Son, 'and I will surely give the nations as Your inheritance, and the very ends of the earth as Your possession.'"*

CHAPTER TWO

PRAYER WARRIORS

In our rapidly changing times people are desperate to know the future. Barely do we adjust to the last changes, when totally new realities explode into our world.

In answer to the common fears spawned by change, society has seen a plethora of occult and demonic sources—fortunetellers, astrologers and psychic hotlines—all pretending to be able to peek into the mystery of tomorrow. Indeed, how many otherwise intelligent individuals glimpse, at least occasionally, at their "astrological signs" trying to get an edge on knowing the future!

Why anyone would consult someone who can't predict their own future is beyond me. These fortunetellers almost always live in abject poverty. Shouldn't their ability to predict the future at least work for themselves? They could invest in the stock market or pick the right lottery numbers. They can't even predict or better their own fortune, yet people go to them for discernment.

TREMENDOUS POWER IN A CHRISTIAN!

For Christians, God condemns this demonic, fleshly probing into the unknown. Indeed, as intercessors, He has called us not to wonder about the future, but to create it through the knowledge of His living Word and prayer! Our Father gives us access to the future right now. You ask, "How do we know what to pray?" The Lord Jesus told us plainly,

> "Pray, then, in this way: 'Our Father who is in heaven, Hallowed be Your name. Your kingdom come. Your will be done, on earth as it is in heaven.' "   —Matthew 6:9–10

We can look at the conditions of the world and faint or look at the possibilities of God and take faith. To bring revival is to pray for the reality of God's kingdom to manifest on earth. Jesus was not offering His disciples a millennial prayer focus, for that rule of God's kingdom is coming whether we want it to or not! No, but Christ calls us to pray for God's kingdom to manifest in our world today.

How will tomorrow look if God answers the prayer Christ gave us? Read the gospels. What we see in the life and power of Jesus Christ is a faith picture of God's kingdom. Jesus said that we can have that same full manifestation. In fact, He actually commanded us to pray for heaven's release!

THE PRAYER WOMB

The reality God has planned will always manifest first in the prayer life of His intercessors. When you hear from God and then pray His Word, you are impacting the unformed essence of life with the Spirit of God Himself!

Thus, God calls us, not only to know His Word, but to pray it. We must go from intellectualizing God's Word to being impregnated by it.

I know churches have special areas where intercessors can pray or people meditate. But maybe we ought to change the name from "prayer room" to "prayer womb." For everything good and holy that we see manifested in people, in churches and in life is first conceived, and then birthed, in the womb of prayer.

We have answers to prayer all around us. The place you are living in is an answer to prayer. Your church is an answer to prayer, as well as are your pastors, teachers and youth workers. As a church member, your attendance and participation is an answer to the prayer of your pastors, leaders and intercessors. When you asked God to lead you to the church you should attend, your current church became God's answer to your prayer!

Paul wrote,

> I pray that the eyes of your heart may be enlightened, so that you may know what is the hope of His calling, what are the riches of the glory of His inheritance in the saints, and what is the surpassing greatness of His power toward us who believe. These are in accordance with the working of the strength of His might.
> —Ephesians 1:18–19

If you are a Christian, there is a power accompanying your life that is greater than great: the "surpassing greatness of His power." It is not human power, but the actual "strength of His might."

Think about it: The strength of God Almighty is attached to your prayer life!

The power of God's might is His resurrection power. What does resurrection mean? It means that things which look dead, smell dead, and act dead, can be touched by God and raised to life!

God demonstrated this "power toward us who believe" first "in Christ, when He raised Him from the dead and seated Him at His right hand in the heavenly places" (Eph 1:20).

Right now, you have resurrection power attached to your prayer life! You can look on things that are absolutely dead and pray forth eternal life!

The power in us is the same potency God demonstrated when He raised Jesus out of the grave; it is resurrection power. Our mission is to bring resurrection life to situations that are dead.

If the devil challenges your prayer, remind him that you are seated with Christ, "far above all rule and authority and power and dominion, and every name that is named, not only in this age but also in the one to come" (Eph 1:21). Christ's authority is final. But not only has the Father put "all things in subjection under His feet"; He "gave Him as head over all things to the church, which is His body, the fullness of Him who fills all in all" (Eph 1:22–23).

Notice the Lord uses anatomical metaphors to explain the downlink of authority: Christ is the "head" of a "body" that has all things put under its "feet."

This is a most profound understanding of our role: What the Head, Christ, has attained, the feet of the church walk out. In other words, God has positioned the church as the living bridge between the terrible conditions on earth and the wonderful solutions from heaven!

As we truly, passionately, and accurately submit to Christ in prayer, the kingdom of heaven steadily enters our now-prayed-for world. The key, of course, is to know Christ's Word. We do not have authority; Christ has authority. What we have is revelation and submission. But as we submit to the Word, and persevere in prayer, the future is impacted and conformed to God's will.

You may have a low self image or struggle with physical problems, but in the Spirit you are very dangerous! The devil knows if he can keep your prayer silent, he keeps God's hand distant. This is why Satan seeks to get you hung up on non-issues.

ARISE, PRAYER WARRIORS!

Jesus told a parable to show that men ought to pray at all times and not lose heart (see Luke 18:1–8). In other words, if you are not praying, you will lose heart. Most of the things I pray for I have to pray through to get the answer. God desires to see something deeper come out of my prayer time than just answered prayers. He wants me to become like Jesus. So He arranges battles that are character-forming; not only will they ultimately change the world around me, but they'll change me first. This is what all true prayer warriors have discovered.

When we picture a prayer warrior, we see a great aunt or grandmother. I think that every family has one. You never find them looking into a crystal ball to know the future for little Johnny—they are at the throne of God creating Johnny's future in prayer. They are not wondering if Mary is going to make it, they are praying her through to victory. They do not have time to lament Harry's drinking problem, they are storming heaven to see him delivered.

Prayer warriors are the most frightening, powerful, demon chasing, world-moving, beings on earth. In truth, they are co-creators with God! If they were to gaze at a crystal ball, it would explode! They look at astrological predictions and rebuke them. They never wonder about the future because they are too busy creating it. Prayer warriors are positioned by God to stand in faith for their family. Prayer is stronger than kings and mightier than armies. Prayer is the most powerful force on earth!

I remember when my dad came to the Lord. For ten years we would intellectually clash about God during our annual visits. Finally, he came "armed" with an argument many use against God. He said, "If there really is a God, why doesn't He always answer prayer?" He was secure in his position and I was tired of the argument. I went into the bathroom and prayed, "Lord, you've got to give me an answer."

When I returned I could see my dad felt he had "won" this round. I love my dad very, very much, but I said, "Dad, forget all the people that you think didn't get answers to prayer—you yourself are an answer to prayer! You are alive today because our entire family daily prays for you." Then I continued, "But let's experiment. You say God doesn't answer prayer; we say He does. So, for one week we won't pray for you, and we'll see what happens."

I can't remember ever seeing my dad turn so pale. He looked over at my mom and said, "Hon, tell the boy not to do that." Then, with beads of sweat forming on his forehead, he said to me, "Okay. What do I have to do to keep you praying for me?"

In three minutes, he went from not believing in prayer to begging us to keep praying for him. I said, "Dad, the only way I'll keep praying for you is if you pray right now and give your life to Christ." The Lord answered my prayer.

Prayer anchors us in God's strength for our battles. Each of us knows prayer works, as we are saved today because someone else prayed for us. Thus, looking at the miracle of our own conversion, we gain confidence in God's help to transform others.

Luke 21:36 tells us to be "praying that you may have strength to escape all these things that are about to take place, and to stand before the Son of Man." He's not talking about the Rapture. Every time the Bible talks about standing before God, it is speaking of a position of anointed authority and commissioning. One who stands before God is an attendant to the Almighty. When they decree God's Word, it comes to pass.

NOTHING IS IMPOSSIBLE!

God has called you to be a prayer warrior. Christ is in you and He ever lives to make intercession. All you need to do is open your heart to Him and prayer is going to come forth. Look at the landscape of life. Every need you see is where God wants you to release, through prayer, His future for that situation. God shows you what is wrong so you can pray for things to be made right. Why waste your energy criticizing what's wrong when your prayer can change it!

The Lord our God in the midst of us is mighty. Our weapons are mighty to pulling down strongholds. Stop thinking of yourself as unable to pray. That's a lie out of hell. You are a prayer warrior!

There was a time when that great aunt or grandmother was younger. She was just like you, and God showed her the needs around her. His grace came and she made a decision not to judge, but to pray. She didn't start off strong, but she became strong. Now it's your turn to make that decision to be the prayer warrior for your family, church or city.

Let's pray: *Lord Jesus, You said that the armies in heaven follow You, and Your name is called "the Word of God." Help me to not only believe Your Word, but pray it in the power of the Holy Spirit! I accept that You have called me to be a prayer warrior. By Your grace, I receive a new anointing in intercession. Amen!*

—FROM THE *ICIT* WEEKLY MAILER

SELF TEST, CHAPTER TWO

Remember, we are looking for answers that correspond with this training. Please write out your essay answers, allowing the Holy Spirit to provoke your thoughts. You may want to use them for group discussion. Note: we do not provide answers to essay questions. To check your multiple choice answers, see answer key in the next session.

Chapter 2, Essay #1: How can I deepen my knowledge of His living Word and prayer, so I can help create the future? *Faith - stop judging - believe that all my prayers are answered*

Chapter 2, Essay #2: There are answers to prayer all around us. In what ways do I see God answering prayer in my life? *So many ways - everyday - blessings, safety, healing, fellowships....*

1. In Matthew 6:9–10, where Jesus instructed us how to pray, what is He actually calling us to pray for?
   a. the hopeless conditions of the world
   b. God's kingdom to manifest in our world today
   c. for more Christian art to come forth
   d. He was giving prayer direction specifically for that time in history

2. If we are praying for God's kingdom to come on earth, what are we to have faith for?
   a. the same full manifestation we see in the life and power of Jesus Christ
   b. occasional breakthroughs after we have been praying long enough
   c. low clouds and rain
   d. all the above

3. Everything good and holy that we see manifested in people, in churches and in life is first conceived, and then birthed, where?
   a. at conferences
   b. in leadership meetings
   c. in prayer
   d. in our financial status

4. What is attached to your prayer life?
   a. responsibility based on our own strength
   b. the strength of God Almighty!
   c. His resurrection power
   d. both b & c

5. If the devil challenges our prayers, what can we do?
   a. back off
   b. be quieter in our prayer life
   c. remind him that we are seated with Christ
   d. yell louder

6. Why does God have us go through such battles and pray so much to get an answer?
   a. He desires to see something deeper come out of our prayer time
   b. So our character can be formed, to become like Jesus
   c. He's waiting to see what He wants to do
   d. both a & b

7. A prayer warrior is not found wondering about the future but rather:
   a. lamenting over those who have needs
   b. checking sources that might tell the future
   c. creating the future in prayer and the knowledge of God's Word
   d. both b & c

8. God shows you what is wrong so you can:
   a. release, through prayer, His future for that situation
   b. confront and bring immediate correction
   c. tell as many others as possible to pray
   d. avoid that situation

Session Two:

Intercession and Protection

For Our Families

SESSION TWO AUDIO MESSAGES:

2a. The Value of Prayer
2b. When You Have Done All, Stand

ANSWER KEY TO LAST SESSION'S
SELF TEST QUESTIONS:

CHAPTER ONE. Ask of Me
1.a, 2.d, 3.b, 4.d, 5.c, 6.d, 7.d, 8.b.
CHAPTER TWO. Prayer Warriors
1.b, 2.a, 3.c, 4.d, 5.c, 6.d, 7.c, 8.a.

CHAPTER THREE

YOUR CHILDREN WILL RETURN

by Joy Frangipane

No one can tell me that fathers and daughters can't have close relationships, or even become best friends. People are almost envious of the love my dad and I share. The only time we argue is about who loves who the most. But our relationship was not always this warm. There was a time when I felt I had lost my ability to love my father. I was a teenage Christian in a public high school. My Christian background made me different. I was new, craving acceptance. My father's rules seemed to be the source of my rejections.

Fueled by my insecurities, in my eyes my dad became the root of my problems. While I set an adequate standard and struggled to live by it, he was strict. I was angry because he refused to back down from the standard he knew was right. He refused to appeal to my ignorance in order to keep my acceptance.

Things were going from bad to worse during those years. We hit bottom the day I looked him square in the eyes and told him that I hated him. They were harsh words, but it was a hard time. I didn't really hate him. I hated me. I felt I wasn't bad enough to be accepted by my friends and not good enough to be accepted at home. When these feelings take over your life, you search for something—anything—to blame. I chose my father. He carried the brunt of my pain. He even became my enemy.

In my heart I knew I didn't hate him. I was angry and confused. I felt he wasn't concerned with how I felt. It seemed he had made no room for compromise with my situation. He risked losing my love to save my soul.

It was a hard time for both of us. He suffered the pain of rejection as I did. He suffered the hurt and the loss, but from a different angle. His fear of the Lord withstood his fear of pain. He loved me, but he had a higher obligation than my favor and my approval. I'm sure at times he wondered if he was doing the right thing. There must have been times when he felt like his prayers were hitting the ceiling and bouncing back at his feet.

At times I'm sure he considered lowering his standards. It would have made things so much easier than wrestling with the power of an independent, strong-willed child. These considerations may have come, but he never gave in to them. He stood firm and prayed harder.

The prayers of a righteous man availeth much. Many times he cried out to the Lord in anguish and in frustration, *"What have I done wrong?"* My father has a wonderful ministry to God in prayer. I think I had something to do with the character God worked in him during those days. Before he ever prayed for cities and nations he was on his face praying for me.

"Train up a child in the way he should go, Even when he is old he will not depart from it" (Prov 22:6). That verse was a promise that he would hold on to. "Your sons and your daughters shall prophesy" (Acts 2:17) was another promise he stood upon.

He had given me to the Lord, set a godly standard and held God to His Word.

At the same time, I was wrestling with my salvation. My desire to be accepted by my non-Christian friends at school warred against my desire to be with the Lord. James speaks of a double-minded person being unstable in all of their ways (see James 1:8). I was completely unstable. I walked on a line between heaven and hell. I wanted the best of both worlds and was satisfied in neither.

Although I had been brought up in the church, the world had taken its toll on me. My eyes had been blinded to the sin in my own life, further separating me from God and parents. It was so hard for me to see my way out.

When a child is brought up in a Christian home, regardless of what may happen, there is a seed that has been planted in their hearts that continues to grow. It's an amazing seed because it can grow in the dark without water; it can even bloom in adversity. The reason we can never outrun God is because He is that seed growing within us. Once you have tasted the presence of the Lord, nothing satisfies you like He can. Sometimes those who seem to be running the hardest from God are doing so because He is so close to them.

On the outside, my witness was weak and I was in bondage to my unsaved friends. But inside my heart cried for oneness with the Lord. I hated my double-mindedness as much as my father did. My whole life I wanted strong Christian friends to save the world with me. I wanted the support, I just never had it. I did the best I could with what I had, but I lost my sensitivity to sin. The more I was with non-Christian people the more deceived I became.

Paul warns, "Do not be bound together with unbelievers; for what partnership have righteousness and lawlessness, or what fellowship has light with darkness?" (2 Cor 6:14) I didn't realize the impact my unsaved friends had on me. The more I was with them the more I conformed to them. When I look back, I know if my parents had not been praying for me, I would have been on my way to hell.

Sin has a way of moving in and taking control. But love is as strong as death, and many waters cannot quench love (see Song 8:6–7). Love never fails (see 1 Cor 13:8). And prayer is the highest power through which love is released. I had to relearn how to love. My love had become completely self-centered and conditional. I had failed to realize that my father and my Lord loved me unconditionally. I had only to try. I had only to bridge the communication gap to understand that God had loved me before I was even aware of His standards. And my dad loved me for me alone, not for something I had to become.

My relationship with my father is wonderful, and that's the truth. God has proven faithful in the working of both our lives. The Lord has bridged the gap and filled it with love. It took me leaving my environment and being planted with Christian people who faithfully loved me. It also took my will to change, but it did happen.

Listen, please don't give up on your teenagers. Don't sacrifice God's standards of righteousness to appeal to their carnal nature. They can't respect you for it and God won't honor it. Your children were not consecrated to Satan; they were dedicated to the Lord. He has had His hand on them and He will not forget them. He has heard your prayers and He is faithful to your cries. He is God.

Prayer works. I'm living proof of it. I look back now and see how many times nothing but the miraculous dedication of loving parents took me out of hopeless situations. The Lord will not forsake His children. He will not turn His back on them. We are never too far from His reach. Believe the promises of the Lord. He is not a liar. He honors a steadfast heart.

Hold on! Your children will come back to the Lord.

Let's pray: *Heavenly Father, help us to never give up on our children. Lord, You said Your Word would not return to You void without accomplishing the purpose for which You sent it. You promised to pour out Your Spirit on our sons and daughters. We ask for our children, even the children of our generation. Bring them into Your kingdom, I pray. In Jesus' name.*

—FROM THE *ICIT* WEEKLY MAILER
JOY FRANGIPANE

SELF TEST, CHAPTER THREE

Remember, we are looking for answers that correspond with this training. Please write out your essay answers, allowing the Holy Spirit to provoke your thoughts. You may want to use them for group discussion. Note: we do not provide answers to essay questions. To check your multiple choice answers, see answer key in the next session.

Chapter 3, Essay #1: Give an example from your life in which you saw prayer change a relationship with a family member or friend. *prayer for people I love has made me more patient & compassionate*

Chapter 3, Essay #2: How do we give our loved ones to the Lord, set a godly standard, and hold God to His Word? *prayer example prayer*

1. What did Francis risk when he made no room for compromise with his daughter Joy's situation?
   a. helping her get what she wanted
   b. losing her love to save her soul
   c. their relationship getting too close
   d. spoiling her

2. When we have a higher obligation than finding favor or approval from man, _____.
   a. our fear of the Lord withstands our fear of the pain of rejection
   b. we can stop praying
   c. it will matter more to us what our children think
   d. we can avoid rejection

3. What is Francis' example to us after being in a place of considering lowering his standards as he wrestled with the power of a strong-willed child?
   a. let others take responsibility for praying
   b. stand firm and pray harder
   c. be still and let them go their way
   d. give in to their most important desires

4. What did Francis prayerfully do at the same time his daughter, Joy, wrestled with her salvation?
   a. continued to give her to the Lord
   b. continued to set a godly standard
   c. held God to His Word
   d. all the above

5. What is the seed planted in the heart and growing within a child brought up in a Christian home?
   a. a watermelon seed we swallowed when we were young
   b. a hope that gets trampled out in adversity
   c. God Himself
   d. a promise that can only grow if watered sufficiently

6. Looking back, what does Joy now realize kept her from the impact her unsaved friends had on her?
   a. her maturity and independence
   b. her strength
   c. her parents praying for her
   d. her friends' loyalty

7. Joy's testimony is proof that
   a. prayer works
   b. the Lord will not forsake His children
   c. God honors a steadfast heart
   d. all the above

8. Joy now advises parents, "_____ _____ to appeal to your teenager's carnal nature."
   a. Don't sacrifice God's standards of righteousness
   b. Fit in with the youth generation
   c. Quit attending AARP meetings
   d. Buy a boom box

QUOTE:

"Prayer is the highest power through which love is released."

CHAPTER FOUR

LEGAL PROTECTION

FAITH IS MORE THAN DOCTRINES

Approximately two thousand years ago a decree was issued from the judgment seat of God. It provided "legal" protection for the church against the devil. Indeed, when Jesus died for our sins, the "ruler of this world" was judged. Our debts were nailed to Christ's cross and canceled; principalities and powers were disarmed (see John 16:11; Col 2:13–15). Because of Jesus, we have a legal right not only to be protected from our enemy but to triumph over him.

The sacrifice of Christ was so complete and the judicial decision from God against Satan so decisive that divine protection, enough to cover even the entire church in a city, has been granted.

Christ's death is the lawful platform upon which the church rises to do spiritual warfare; His Word is the eternal sword we raise against wickedness. Having said that, we must also acknowledge that the church has only rarely walked in such victory since the first century. Why? The answer is this: To attain the protection of Christ, the church must embrace the intercession of Christ. We must become a house of prayer.

Indeed, church history began with its leadership devoted to the Word of God and to prayer (see Acts 2:42; 6:4). Every day the leaders gathered to pray and minister to the Lord (see Acts 3:1). In this clarity of vision and simplicity of purpose, the church of Jesus Christ never had greater power or capacity to make true disciples. These men and women revealed the purity of the kingdom of God.

Today, however, our qualifications for church leadership include almost everything but devotion to God's Word and prayer. Leaders are expected to be organizers, counselors, and individuals with winning personalities whose charms alone can draw people.

In Luke 18:8, Jesus challenges our modern traditions. He asks, "When the Son of Man comes, will He find faith on the earth?" His question is a warning to Christians who would limit the power of God at the end of the age. Jesus is calling us to resist the downward pull of our traditions; He is asking us as individuals, "Will I find faith in you?"

Before we respond, let us note that Jesus associates "faith" with "day and night prayer" (Luke 18:7). He is not asking, "Will I find correct doctrines in you?" The Lord's question does not so much concern itself with right knowledge as with right faith. What we believe is important, but how we believe is vital in securing the help of God.

Indeed, procuring the supernatural help of God is exactly the point of Jesus' parable in Luke 18. His intent was to show that "at all times" we "ought to pray and not to lose heart" (Luke 18:1). To illustrate the quality of faith He seeks, He followed His admonition with a parable about a certain widow who petitioned a hardened judge for "legal protection" (v 3). Although the judge was initially unwilling, yet by her "continually coming" (v 5) she gained what was legally hers.

Jesus concluded by saying if an unrighteous judge will respond to a widow's persistence, shall not God avenge quickly "His elect who cry to Him day and night, and will He delay long over them?" Jesus said, "I tell you that He will bring about justice for them speedily" (see Luke 18:1–8).

Understanding God's Delays

Our Heavenly Judge will not delay long over His elect, but He will delay. In fact, God's definition of "speedily" and ours are not always synonymous. The Lord incorporates delays into His overall plan: Delays work perseverance in us. So crucial is endurance to our character development that God is willing to delay even important answers to prayer to facilitate our transformation.

Thus, we should not interpret divine delays as signs of divine reluctance. Delays are tools to perfect our faith. Christ is looking to find a tenacity in our faith that prevails in spite of delays and setbacks. He seeks to create a perseverance within us that outlasts the test of time, a resolve that actually grows stronger during delays. When the Father sees this quality of persistence in our faith, it so touches His heart that He grants "legal protection" to His people.

Desperation Produces Change

It is significant that Jesus compared His elect to a widow harassed by an enemy. The image is actually liberating, for we tend to conceptualize the heroes of the faith as David or Joshua types—individuals whose successes obscure their humble beginnings. But each of God's servants has, like the widow, a former life that is brimming with excuses and occasions to waver.

Look at the widow: She has legitimate reasons to quit, but instead she prevails. Indeed, she refuses to exempt herself from her high potential simply because of her lowly estate. She makes no apologies for her lack of finances, knowledge or charm. Giving herself no reason to fail, she unashamedly plants her case before the judge where she pleads for and receives what is hers: legal protection from her opponent.

How did a common widow gain such strength of character? We can imagine that there must have been a time when, under the relentless pressure of her adversary, she became desperate—and desperation worked to her advantage. Desperation is God's hammer: It demolishes the stronghold of fear and shatters the chains of our excuses. When desperation exceeds our fears, progress begins.

Today, the force prodding many Christians toward greater unity and prayer has not been the sweetness of fellowship; more often it has been the assault of the enemy. We are in desperate times. When it comes to touching God's heart, other than for a few essential truths, unity of desperation is more crucial than unity of doctrine.

Consider the degree of our national moral decline: In the time it takes to read this, ten babies will be aborted in America. Based on current statistics, this year there will be an estimated 34 million crimes committed. Of those, nearly 600,000 will be violent crimes, and 72% of that number will be against our teenagers. In what place is a teen most frequently assaulted, raped or murdered today? Most violent acts are committed against teens in their schools!

GOD'S ELECT

Our nation is suffering from a deep social and moral collapse. If we have ever needed God's anointing, it is now—but where are God's elect? Where are the people whom Daniel says "know their God" and "will display strength and take action"? (Dan 11:32)

Is there no one divinely empowered who can fell the Goliaths of our age? Perhaps we are looking in the wrong places. Perhaps we need only to look in our bathroom mirror. If you believe in Jesus and are desperate for God, you qualify as one of God's elect. Remember, in the above parable the widow typifies Christ's chosen.

We have erroneously held that God's chosen will never be assaulted by the adversary, much less driven to desperation and "day and night" prayer. But, this desperation is often the very crucible in which the elect of God are forged. Jesus portrays this characteristic metaphorically in the picture of the widow; He reveals the means through which His elect prevail in battle at the end of the age.

When all is said and done, it is also possible that this widow may not have been a singular person but a corporate people—a "widow church"—united in Christ in a singular, desperate prayer for protection against her adversary.

We need the "legal protection" that a national revival provides. But it will not come without unceasing prayer. You ask, "Where was the prayer behind the charismatic renewal?" The Lord spoke to my heart that the charismatic renewal was His answer to the cries of a million praying mothers—women who refused to surrender their children to drugs and the devil.

It is our turn to pray. We are the widow who cannot give herself a reason for failure; God will answer our day and night cry. Let us position ourselves at His throne. Certainly, He will grant us legal protection in our cities.

Day and Night Prayer

The spiritual immunity God provides us as individuals has a divinely inspired, built-in limitation: The Spirit of Christ which shelters us from the enemy also makes us vulnerable to the needs of

others. As it is written, "If one member suffers, all the members suffer with it" (1 Cor 12:26). Thus, to perfect love, God unites us to other people; to empower prayer, He allows us to be vicariously identified with the sufferings of those we care for.

If we cease to love, we will fail to pray. Love is the fuel behind all intercession. Are you weary or vacillating in your prayer life? Remember the love God first gave you, whether it was for your family or church, city or nation. Love will identify you with those you love; it will revive your prayer, and prayer will revive your loved ones.

Consider Daniel. Daniel loved Israel. He loved the temple. Although Daniel was not guilty of the sins of Israel, his prayer was an expression of his identification with the nation. Daniel put on sackcloth and ashes and sought the Lord with prayer and supplication. He prayed,

> Alas, O Lord, the great and awesome God, who keeps His covenant and lovingkindness for those who love Him and keep His commandments, we have sinned, committed iniquity, acted wickedly, and rebelled, even turning aside from Thy commandments and ordinances.   —Daniel 9:4–5

Had Daniel sinned? No. But his love and identification with Israel made his repentance legitimate. Additionally, Daniel was faithful in his daily prayer for Israel—he prayed all his life for the restoration of the nation. Consider: After a year or two our faithfulness begins to wane. But Daniel was faithful every day throughout his life!

When Darius passed a law forbidding petitions to any god or man other than himself, Daniel was not intimidated. We read,

> Now when Daniel knew that the writing was signed, he went home. And in his upper room, with his windows open toward Jerusalem, he knelt down on his knees

three times that day, and prayed and gave thanks before his God, as was his custom since early days.   —Daniel 6:10 NKJV

Daniel was one of the first exiles from Israel to Babylon. We can imagine, in the terror and trauma of seeing one's society destroyed and its survivors enslaved and exiled, that Daniel's parents had firmly planted in his young heart Solomon's prayer, which embodied God's requirements for restoration:

> When Thy people Israel are defeated before an enemy, because they have sinned against Thee, if they turn to Thee again and confess Thy name and pray and make supplication to Thee in this house, then hear Thou in heaven, and forgive the sin of Thy people Israel, and bring them back to the land which Thou didst give to their fathers.   —1 Kings 8:33–34

Thus, Daniel prayed three times a day, every day, since his earliest years. He continued in prayer for nearly seventy years, until the time Jeremiah's prophecy came to pass!

You see, the work of God takes time. How long should we pray? We pray as long as it takes. Consider Anna, who ministered to the Lord in prayer and fasting in the temple for approximately sixty years, crying out to God until He sent the Messiah. Or Cornelius, whose "prayers and alms . . . ascended as a memorial before God" (Acts 10:4). We do not understand the responsibility and privilege God places upon a person who continues in faithful prayer. What sustained these champions of prayer? They loved God and loved the people of God.

Costly Lessons

While the work of revival is often initiated through the love and intercession of one person, there is a time when the prayer burden must be picked up and shared by many. It is not enough that God graces one individual to become a man or woman of prayer; the Lord seeks to make His church a house of prayer.

One way or another the plan of God is to make intercessors of us all. We can learn the indispensable priority of prayer directly from God's Word. We can also learn of the need to pray from the victories or mistakes of others. Or, we can learn of the necessity of prayer the hard way: We can fail to pray and let the consequences teach us.

For some, these will be costly lessons. We will not be able to blame the devil if the real culprit was our neglect of prayer. In extreme cases, the Lord will actually allow tragedy to reinforce the urgency and priority of prayer. The following incident from the book of Acts underscores the need to keep our prayer life strong and sensitive to changes in our spiritual battles. The story also reveals that tremendous power is released when the whole church in a city prays.

Of all Jesus' followers, three were considered the "inner circle": Peter, James and John. Yet, Luke tells us of a terrible event in the life of the early Christians: Herod executed the apostle James. Until that time the leaders of the church walked in spiritual protection. However, they failed to discern that the intensity of satanic assault had escalated. The result was that James, an apostle who stood with Christ on the Mount of Transfiguration, was beheaded.

The appalling murder of James shocked the church. How was it that this anointed apostle died so prematurely? Where was God's protection? Perhaps this is the answer: The Lord suppressed His sovereign protection that He might bring the church into intercessory protection.

The death of James pleased the Jews, so Herod imprisoned Peter also, intending to kill him after the Feast of Unleavened Bread. At this point, the Scripture says, "Peter therefore was kept in prison; but prayer was made without ceasing of the church unto God for him" (Acts 12:5 KJV). The NKJV says that "constant prayer" was offered to God; the NIV says the church was praying "earnestly"; the NASB tells us that the church was praying "fervently." Earnest, fervent, constant prayer was made for Peter by the entire church in Jerusalem!

The outcome of this aggressive intercession was that Peter was supernaturally delivered, the guards who held Peter were executed and, a short time later, Herod himself was struck down by an angel of the Lord. When the entire citywide church engaged in continual, day and night prayer, God granted deliverance!

In the many years I have served the Lord, I have known individuals, prayer groups and even denominations which have embraced varying degrees of 24-hour prayer. I have participated with prayer chains and prayer vigils. But I have yet to see an entire, citywide Christian community put aside minor doctrinal differences and take God's promise seriously.

When the local churches in a community truly become a house united in prayer, God will begin to guide the entire church into the shelter of His protection. And, according to Jesus, "He will bring about justice for them speedily" (Luke 18:8).

Let's pray: *Lord God, under the terms of the new covenant, You have provided legal protection for us from our adversary. We come now to Your throne and ask for You to bring justice speedily on our behalf. Bring Your people together in our city to cry, day and night, to You in prayer, until the blessings Jesus purchased are manifest in our lives and our cities. In Jesus' name. Amen.*

—FROM THE BOOK, *THE POWER OF COVENANT PRAYER*

SELF TEST, CHAPTER FOUR

Remember, we are looking for answers that correspond with this training. Please write out your essay answers, allowing the Holy Spirit to provoke your thoughts. You may want to use them for group discussion. Note: we do not provide answers to essay questions. To check your multiple choice answers, see answer key in the next session.

Chapter 4, Essay #1: What is "day and night prayer"? Can you see its value in your life?

prayer is at one / all times

Chapter 4, Essay #2: In what ways are you ready for love to revive your prayer, and that prayer to revive your loved ones?

Not to pray for what I what of someone, that they become what Christ desires. Therefore I can love them

1. What is the lawful platform upon which the church rises to do spiritual warfare?
   a. the stage
   b. the court system
   c. Christ's death
   d. our righteousness

2. What must the church do to attain the protection of Christ and to triumph over our enemy?
   a. embrace the intercession of Christ
   b. become a house of prayer
   c. overpower any opposition
   d. both a & b

3. In following the example of the early church in Acts, moving in power and making true disciples, our qualifications for church leadership today need to be:
   a. devotion to God's Word and prayer
   b. having a personality that charms people
   c. counseling skills
   d. the gift of administration

4. In Luke 18:7–8, where Jesus says God will avenge His elect who cry to Him, Jesus is associating "faith" with:
   a. knowing what we want
   b. day and night prayer
   c. knowing correct doctrines
   d. being regular in attending church

5. Like the widow pleading her case to the judge, we ought to pray and not lose heart, and refuse to exempt ourselves from our _____ simply because of our lowly estate.
   a. freedom
   b. legal protection
   c. high potential
   d. both b & c

6. When it comes to touching God's heart, other than for a few essential truths, what is more crucial than unity of doctrine?
   a. unity of desperation
   b. unity of language
   c. unity of our teachings
   d. all the above

7. The execution of James in Acts underscores the need for all intercessors to keep our prayer life strong and:
   a. take frequent breaks from ministry
   b. correct one another when praying out of God's will
   c. stay focused within our particular denomination
   d. be sensitive to discerning when the intensity of satanic assault escalates

8. What must happen for God to truly guide the church into the shelter of His protection and bring about justice speedily?
   a. more classes and teachings
   b. double helpings of chicken at church picnics
   c. local churches unite and become a citywide house of prayer
   d. keep on as we are

Luke 19:1-10

> **QUOTE:**
>
> *"If we cease to love, we will fail to pray. Love is the fuel behind all intercession."*

E nemies harassing
L egitimate reason to quit
E xcuses + Fears
C haracter yielded to God
T ouching God's heart

SESSION THREE:

THE POWER OF ONE

James 5:19-20
1 Peter 4:8
Genesis 9:23

Chapter Five

One Man

A familiar statement in American Christianity and a popular quote that has been prevalent for the last few years is, "If God doesn't destroy America, He will have to apologize to Sodom and Gomorrah." I have heard this comment repeated in churches and revival meetings; it was actually quoted by secular newspapers, epitomizing the Christian perspective expounded at political conventions.

For most, this remark is simply a clever or emphatic way of saying that America needs to repent, and that, as a nation, Americans are in danger of invoking God's wrath. Within this rhetorical sphere, the expression certainly has its value, and a number of Christians have repeated it with this intent. In fact, for a while I used it myself in this rhetorical sense.

But the Holy Spirit began to check me about repeating this view of America. First, because it isn't really true (a majority of Americans are not violent homosexuals); second, because God has been doing something wonderful in our land, uniting Christians and raising up an ever resurgent prayer movement that is integral to the divine plan. We are moving in a direction different from wrath, which the Lord not only recognizes, but also has inspired.

Spark of Hope
Intercession
Not responding
in the flesh –
Co-operate
w/ God
Observe His Character
Value human life
Expand your expectation
Reveal
(Christ Redemption)

Yet, when I questioned a number of church leaders about this "God-about-to-destroy-America" attitude, I was amazed to discover that a majority actually believed this statement not to be rhetorical, but true. In their eyes, America was worse than Sodom and Gomorrah. As I probed, I uncovered a deep bitterness in a number of leaders toward the United States. In fact, because I did not share the deep-seated bitterness of one colleague toward the United States, I was questioned as to whether I had compromised my stand on holiness!

The true measure of spirituality is not how angry we become toward sinners, but how Christlike; our mission is not to see men destroyed, but redeemed.

For the sake of illustration, let us assume my colleague's view is correct, that this nation is as evil as Sodom. In the historical account, Sodom and Gomorrah present the pattern of wickedness, but let's also examine the pattern of righteousness in the story. Let's look at how Abraham responded to God's warning of imminent destruction.

GOD'S RESPONSE TO MERCIFUL INTERCESSION

When Abraham was confronted with the possibility of Sodom's destruction, he did not immediately jump on the "Destroy Sodom" bandwagon; instead, he went before the Lord and prayed for mercy for the city. Abraham's prayer is an amazing study on the effect a mercy-motivated intercessor has on the heart of God. My object here is to look past this event and gaze into the heart of God, which is revealed in the discourse between the Lord and Abraham.

As we look at Abraham's prayer, we discover the key, the power we have in intercession. We discover the element the Lord is seeking in providing us the privilege of prayer. And what is that? He is looking for a spark of hope within us, for us to recognize a mercy reason that would justify delaying or canceling wrath. We must not belittle this principle, for in it is great hope for our land as well.

Let us consider also the Lord's initial response to Sodom's sin. First, He revealed to Abraham, His servant, what He was about to do. Why? Because God desired Abraham to intercede.

When the Lord informed His servant of what was wrong in the world, it was not so that Abraham could simply criticize it, but so that he would intercede for mercy. Remember, God delights in mercy (see Micah 7:18) and takes "no pleasure in the death of the wicked" (Ezek 33:11). The Lord always seeks for opportunities of mercy. Therefore, let's take note of how Abraham approached the Almighty:

> Then the men turned away from there and went toward Sodom, while Abraham was still standing before the Lord. And Abraham came near and said, "Wilt Thou indeed sweep away the righteous with the wicked? Suppose there are fifty righteous within the city; wilt Thou indeed sweep it away and not spare the place for the sake of the fifty righteous who are in it?
>
> "Far be it from Thee to do such a thing, to slay the righteous with the wicked, so that the righteous and the wicked are treated alike. Far be it from Thee! Shall not the Judge of all the earth deal justly?"
>
> —Genesis 18:22–25

No Compromise with Sin

Notice, Abraham did not pray from a place of anger. He never said, "God, it's about time You killed the perverts." There was no finger-pointing vindictiveness in Abraham's soul. Somehow, we have come to believe that non-compromising Christians must also be angry. Abraham never compromised with Sodom's depraved culture, yet he was above fleshly reaction. In fact, throughout his prayer, Abraham never mentioned what was wrong in Sodom. He appealed, instead, to the mercy and integrity of the Lord.

This is vitally important for us, because Jesus said, "If you are Abraham's children, do the deeds of Abraham" (John 8:39). One of Abraham's most noteworthy deeds involved his intercessory prayer for Sodom, the most perverse city in the world!

Abraham first acknowledged the Lord's integrity, then he spoke to the Lord's mercy. "Suppose there are fifty righteous within the city; wilt Thou indeed sweep it away and not spare the place for the sake of the fifty righteous who are in it?" (Gen 18:24).

The Lord knew that it would be unjust to slay the righteous with the wicked; Abraham's prayer did not enlighten the Lord of some unknown fact. But the nature of life on earth is this: God works with man to establish the future and, in the process of determining reality, He always prepares a merciful alternative.

In other words, urgent, redemptive prayer shoots straight through the mercy door and enters God's heart. This door is never shut, especially since we have a High Priest, Jesus Christ, ministering at the mercy seat in the heavens (see Heb 8:1). It is open each and every time we pray. Listen to how the Lord answered Abraham's prayer for mercy: "If I find in Sodom fifty righteous within the city, then I will spare the whole place on their account" (Gen 18:26).

How the truth of God's mercy flies in the face of those so eager to judge their nation! Incredibly, the Lord said He would spare the whole of Sodom if He found fifty righteous people there. Now, keep this in mind: an alternate rendering for the Hebrew word for "spare" means "to forgive or pardon." When there is Christ-inspired prayer offered for sinners, the Lord will minimize, delay, or even cancel the exercise of His wrath!

GOD'S ABUNDANT LOVE

Time and again throughout the Scriptures the Lord proclaims an ever present truth about His nature: He is "slow to anger, and abounding in lovingkindness" (Exod 34:6). Do we believe this? Here it is, demonstrated right before our eyes in the Scriptures. He tells us plainly that a few righteous people scattered in a city can preserve that area from divine wrath.

Abraham knew the love of God. He was an intimate friend of God's. Abraham, in truth, had a clear view into the heart of God based on his own experiences. This interceding patriarch had seen the Almighty bless, prosper, and forgive him, so he pressed God's mercy toward its limits.

"What if there are forty?"

The Lord would spare it for forty.

Abraham bargained, "Thirty?"

He would spare it for thirty.

"Twenty?"

He finally secured the Lord's promise not to destroy the city if He could find just ten righteous people there. On God's scales, put the entire city of Sodom with all its sin and perversion on one side. On the side of wrath is the weightiness of advanced wickedness run rampant through a complete city. Let's assume that there were 200,000 evil people in Sodom. It is weighed heavily on the side of evil. Yet, on the other side, place just ten righteous individuals. As the ten are placed on the scale, the spiritual weight of the righteous, with just ten, tips the scales toward mercy.

In God's heart, the substance of the righteous far outweighs the wickedness of the evil! Herein we discover what we are seeking in the heart of God through prayer: the Lord would spare (forgive) sinful Sodom, with its gangs of violent homosexuals, because of the influence of ten godly people who dwelt within it!

HOW ABOUT YOUR COMMUNITY?

Now, let's think of your city: are there ten good people among you? Consider your region. Do you think there might be one hundred praying people living within its borders, people who are pleading with God for mercy? What about nationwide? Do you suppose there might be ten thousand people interceding for your country? God said He would spare Sodom for ten righteous people. Do you think God would spare your nation for ten thousand righteous?

I live in a metropolitan area in the United States that has about two hundred thousand people. I can list by name scores of righteous individuals, including pastors, intercessors, youth workers, black folks, white folks, Hispanic folks, Native Americans, Asian Americans, Christian business people, moms, dads, godly teenagers, praying grandmothers, secretaries, policemen, and on and on, who live here—far more than the ten righteous needed to save a place like Sodom. Many here care about this city.

Think about your church and the greater church community in your city. Aren't there at least ten honorable people who sincerely care about your community, who desire that God would bring revival? Remember, the Lord said He would spare Sodom for the sake of the ten.

GOD'S LOVE FOR THE RIGHTEOUS

One last thought concerning Abraham and Sodom: when the Lord's messengers came to rescue Lot and his family, Lot hesitated. Pressured by two of God's avenging angels to flee to the mountains, Lot asked that he and his family might instead escape to Zoar. As one of the angels granted his request, God's messenger uttered something amazing. The angel said, "Hurry, escape there, for I cannot do anything until you arrive there" (Gen 19:22).

"I cannot do anything." Think about this, my friends: God had put a limitation on His wrath! As long as the righteous dwelt in the city, it was protected. Indeed, when Lot fled to Zoar, though fire and brimstone fell and consumed every inhabitant of every community in the valley, Zoar was protected without a single casualty. Why? Because the righteous were there.

Just One

Abraham stopped his prayer at ten people. But I will tell you something that is most profound: man of faith that he was, Abraham stopped praying too soon. The Lord reveals in Scripture that His mercy will extend even further. The scene is sinful Jerusalem. Yet, listen to what the Almighty told Jeremiah:

> Roam to and fro through the streets of Jerusalem, and look now, and take note. And seek in her open squares, if you can find a man, if there is one who does justice, who seeks truth, then I will pardon her.   —Jeremiah 5:1

He says, "If you can find a man . . . who does justice . . . then I will pardon [Jerusalem]." One holy person in an unholy city can actually turn away God's wrath. One godly individual who remains righteous while living among the ungodly, who cares for a community or a family or a school or a neighborhood or a church, swings open the door for mercy.

My friends, it is not a little thing to God that He has a soul that remains righteous in an unrighteous world. If just one heart refuses to give in to the intimidation of increasing wickedness, if that one refuses to submit to hopelessness, fear, or unbelief, it is enough to exact from heaven a delay of wrath. You, my friend, can be that one who obtains forgiveness for your city, who stands between the godless past and a God-filled future!

Mercy far outweighs wrath. Mercy always triumphs over judgment. You see, whenever a person operates in intercessory mercy, the tender passions of Christ are unveiled in the world. Do you truly want to know who Jesus is? Consider this: He ever lives to make intercession (see Heb 7:25); He is seated at the right hand of God the Father, praying on our behalf (see Rom 8:34). He is not waiting in heaven, eagerly desiring an opportunity to destroy the world. He is praying for mercy. This is His nature.

Christ, the second person of the Trinity, is God in His mercy form. He is God, loving the world, dying for its sins, and paying the price of redemption. Christ is the mercy of God satisfying the justice of God.

God declared that man was to be made in the divine image, and it is this image of Christ the Redeemer that reveals our pattern. We are to follow the mercy path set by Christ. The Scriptures boldly declare God's goal for the church: "As He is, so also are we in this world" (1 John 4:17).

Thus, the nature of Christ is manifest in our world every time redemptive intercession is offered to God for sinners. Jesus came to earth to fulfill the mercy of God. His title is Redeemer. His role is Savior. He is the Good Shepherd who "lays down His life for [His] sheep" (John 10:11). God calls us to be like Jesus who, in turn, says to us, "As the Father has sent Me, I also send you" (John

20:21). We are sent by Jesus with the purpose of redemption.

The manifestation on earth of one Christlike intercessor perfectly restrains God's need for judgment on a society. Let me say it again: "Mercy triumphs over judgment" (James 2:13). Mercy corresponds exactly with God's heart. Yes, it is true. One man or woman who reveals Christ's heart on earth will defer God's judgment from heaven.

Let's pray: *Lord Jesus, forgive me for devaluing the power of prayer. Forgive me for underestimating how passionately You desire to reveal Your mercy. Lord, give me grace to be one who never ceases to cry out to You for mercy. Lord, let me not base my obedience on what my eyes see or my ears hear, but upon the revelation of Your mercy; let me build my life on Thee. Amen!*

—FROM THE BOOK, *THE POWER OF ONE CHRISTLIKE LIFE*

SELF TEST, CHAPTER FIVE

Remember, we are looking for answers that correspond with this training. Please write out your essay answers, allowing the Holy Spirit to provoke your thoughts. You may want to use them for group discussion. Note: we do not provide answers to essay questions. To check your multiple choice answers, see answer key in the next session.

Chapter 5, Essay #1: Am I growing in the ability to show mercy, that the tender passions of Christ will be unveiled in the world around me?

I am striving — have a long way to go.

Chapter 5, Essay #2: Do I believe that my prayers can make a difference in the society I live in? *Yes yes yes*
some one prayed me to Christ

1. What dramatic element occurs when we embrace redemptive intercession?
    a. a major win happens at casino gambling
    b. we provide the Almighty with a "mercy reason" that allows Him to delay or even cancel the exercise of His wrath toward sin
    c. we learn to dance in church
    d. we die a more pleasant death

2. What was the Lord's initial response to Sodom's sin?
    a. He began to express His pleasure in destroying the wicked
    b. He became angry even with Abraham His servant

c. He revealed to Abraham what He was about to do, not so Abraham could criticize, but so he would intercede

d. all the above

3. Jesus said, "If you are Abraham's children, do the deeds of Abraham" (John 8:39). What was one of Abraham's most noteworthy deeds?

    a. staying in his own homeland

    b. keeping his blessings for his own family

    c. both a & b

    d. intercessory prayer of mercy for Sodom

4. When the Lord said He would "spare" Sodom if He could find ten righteous people there, what does that reveal about the heart of God?

    a. mercy triumphs over judgment

    b. He sometimes forgets how bad things get down here

    c. He is willing to delay wrath for the sake of a righteous few

    d. both a & c

5. Due to the Lord's response to Abraham's intercession, we can plainly see that a few righteous people in a city can:

    a. survive if they keep a low profile

    b. buy property real cheap after the wicked are destroyed

    c. be the deciding influence in that city's future

    d. make no difference when it comes to judgment of sins

6. According to Jeremiah 5:1, what does it take to open the door of mercy for a city?

    a. a special set of golden keys

    b. one godly individual who remains righteous while living among the ungodly

    c. a door knob on your side of the door

    d. a prophet who can identify every sin in the place

7. On God's scales, what attribute far outweighs wrath and judgment?

    a. service

    b. anger

    c. mercy

    d. having the high score on the church bowling team

8. We are sent by Jesus with the purpose of _____.

    a. redemption

    b. condemning sinners

    c. becoming like Jesus

    d. both a & c

QUOTE:

"The true measure of spirituality is not how angry we become toward sinners, but how Christlike; our mission is not to see men destroyed, but redeemed."

Session Four:

The Word at War

SESSION FOUR AUDIO MESSAGES:

4a. Crushed by God (part 1)
4b. Crushed by God (part 2)

ANSWER KEY TO LAST SESSION'S
SELF TEST QUESTIONS:

CHAPTER FIVE. One Man
1.b, 2.c, 3.d, 4.d, 5.c, 6.b, 7.c, 8.d.

CHAPTER SIX

EXPOSING THE ACCUSER OF THE BRETHREN

More churches have been destroyed by the accuser of the brethren and its faultfinding than by either immorality or misuse of church funds. So prevalent is this influence in our society that, among many, faultfinding has been elevated to the status of a "ministry"! The Lord has promised, however, that in His house accusing one another will be replaced with prayer, and faultfinding with a love that covers a multitude of sins.

SATAN WANTS TO STOP YOUR GROWTH

This session is specifically to expose the activity of the accuser of the brethren among born-again Christians. There are individuals who are trapped in cults where mind-control and deception is involved; we are not dealing with the uniqueness of their problems in this study. Rather, our goal is to see the living church delivered from the stronghold of faultfinding, and to have our hearts turned instead to prayer.

In an attempt to hinder, if not altogether halt, the next move of God, Satan has sent forth an army of faultfinding demons against the church. The purpose of this assault is to entice the body of Christ away from the perfections of Jesus and onto the imperfections of one another.

The faultfinder spirit's assignment is to assault relationships on all levels. It attacks families, churches and inter-church associations, seeking to bring irreparable schisms into our unity. Masquerading as discernment, this spirit will slip into our opinions of other people, leaving us critical and judgmental. Consequently, we all need to evaluate our attitude toward others. If our thoughts are other than "faith working through love," we need to be aware that we may be under spiritual attack.

The faultfinder demon will incite individuals to spend days and even weeks unearthing old faults or sins in their minister or church. The people who are held captive by this deceitful spirit become "crusaders," irreconcilable enemies of their former assemblies. In most cases, the things they deem wrong or lacking are the very areas in which the Lord seeks to position them for intercession. What might otherwise be an opportunity for spiritual growth and meeting a need becomes an occasion of stumbling and withdrawal. In truth, their criticisms are a smokescreen for a prayerless heart and an unwillingness to serve.

That someone should discover the imperfections of their pastor, leaders or church is by no means a sign of spirituality. Indeed, we could find fault with the church before we were Christians. What we do with what we see, however, is the measure of Christlike maturity. Remember, when Jesus saw the condition of mankind, He "emptied Himself, taking the form of a bond-servant . . . He humbled Himself by becoming obedient to the point of death, even death on a cross" (Phil 2:7–8). He died to take away sin, He did not just judge them.

Attention Drawn away from the perfection of Christ

It is of some consolation that Christ Himself could not satisfy the "standards" of this spirit when it spoke through the Pharisees. No matter what Jesus did, the Pharisees found fault with Him.

If you personally have not consulted with and listened to the individual of whom you are critical, how can you be sure that you are not fulfilling the role of the accuser of the brethren? Even the "Law does not judge a man, unless it first hears from him" (John 7:51).

The enemy's purpose in this assault is to discredit the minister so it can discredit his message. I have personally listened to scores of pastors from many denominational backgrounds. The timing of this spirit's attack upon their congregations almost always was just prior to, or immediately after, a significant breakthrough. The unchallenged assault of this demon always stopped the forward progress of their church.

When this spirit infiltrates an individual's mind, its accusations come with such venom and intimidation that even those who should "know better" are bewildered and then seduced by its influence. Nearly all involved take their eyes off Jesus and focus upon "issues," ignoring during the contention that Jesus is actually praying for His body to become one. Beguiled by this demon, accusations and counter accusations rifle through the soul of the congregation, stimulating suspicion and fear among the people. Devastation wracks the targeted church, while discouragement blankets and seeks to destroy the pastor and his family, or other servants of God in the church.

Nearly every minister reading this has faced the assault of the faultfinder spirit at one time or another. Each has known the depression of trying to track down this accusing spirit as it whispers its gossip through the local church: trusted friends

Attention Drawn Away (...)
PRAY (About everything)
Effort to Discredit
Strife + inaction
derail the vision of the church

Prayerless heart + unwillingness to serve

seem distant, established relationships are shaken, and the vision of the church is quagmired in strife and inaction.

This enemy is not limited to attacks on local churches, however. Its attacks are also citywide and national. Major publishers have made millions of dollars selling defaming books which are hardly more credible than gossip columns in the tabloids.

Yes, in a few of the ministries there was serious sin, but there are biblical ways to bring correction, ways which lead to healing and not to destruction! There are denominational supervisors, as well as local ministerial associations, that can review disputes privately. Instead, church leaders boldly challenge other leaders; newsletters and cassette tapes critical of various ministries circulate like poison through the bloodstream of the body of Christ—and how the Savior's church gluttonously eats it up!

To mask the diabolical nature of its activity, the faultfinder will often garb its criticisms in religious clothing. Under the pretense of protecting sheep from a "gnat-sized" error in doctrine, it forces the flock to swallow a "camel-sized" error of loveless correction. Attempting to correct violations of Scripture, the very methods employed are a violation of Scripture! Where is the "spirit of gentleness" of which Paul speaks in Galatians 6:1, the humility in "looking to yourselves, lest you too be tempted"? Where is the love motive to "restore such a one"?

In most cases the person supposedly in "error" has never even been contacted before his alleged mistakes enter the rumor mill of the city's churches. Only then, after the slander has been made public through a book, tape or media broadcast does he become aware of his alleged faults. Brethren, the spirit behind such accusations must be discerned, for its motive is not to restore and heal, but to destroy!

THE PURE EXAMPLE

The church does need correction, but the ministry of reproof must be patterned after Christ and not the accuser of the brethren. When Jesus corrected the churches in Asia (see Rev 2–3), He sandwiched His rebuke between praise and promises. He reassured the churches that the Voice about to expose their sin was the very Voice which inspired their virtue. After encouraging them, He then brought correction.

Even when a church was steeped in error, as was the case with two of the seven churches, Christ still offered grace for change. How patient was Jesus? He even gave "Jezebel . . . time to repent"! (Rev 2:20–21) After He admonished a church, His last words were not condemnation, but promises.

Is this not His way with each of us? Even in the most serious corrections, the voice of Jesus is always the embodiment of "grace and truth" (John 1:14). Jesus said of the sheep, "They know his voice. And a stranger they simply will not follow, but will flee from him" (John 10:4–5). Remember, if the word of rebuke or correction does not offer grace for restoration, it is not the voice of your Shepherd. If you are one of Christ's sheep, you will flee from it.

THE ENEMY'S WEAPONS

To find an indictment against the church, it is important to note, the enemy must draw his accusations from hell. If we have repented of our sins, no record of them nor of our mistakes exists in heaven. As it is written, "Who will bring a charge against God's elect? God is the one who justifies" (Rom 8:33). Jesus is not condemning us, but rather is at the Father's right hand interceding on our behalf.

Let us, therefore, expose the weapons of the faultfinder. The first is our actual sins. Our failure

Sins
Past mistakes
Emotions
Waging a campaign against a brother

Emotions of jealousy & fear

to repent when the Holy Spirit desires to correct us opens the door for the accuser to condemn us. The voice of the enemy never offers hope nor extends grace for repentance. It acts as though it were the voice of God, and we were guilty of the "unpardonable sin." The way to defeat the enemy in this arena is to disarm him by <u>sincerely</u> repenting of the sin, looking again to the atonement of Christ as the sum of all our righteousness.

Yet, Satan seeks not only to accuse us as individuals, but to blend into our minds, introducing criticisms and condemnation against others as well. Instead of praying for one another, we react in the flesh against offenses. Our unchristlike responses are then easily manipulated by the faultfinder spirit.

Therefore, we cast down the accuser of the brethren by learning to pray for one another instead of preying on one another. We must learn to forgive in the same manner as Christ has forgiven us. If one has repented of his sins, we must exercise the same attitude of "<u>divine forgetfulness</u>" that exists in heaven. We defeat the faultfinder when we emulate the nature of Jesus: like a lamb, Christ died for sinners; as a priest, He intercedes.

The second weapon this demon uses against us is our past mistakes and poor decisions. Each of us has an inherent propensity toward ignorance. One does not have to read far into the history of the saints to discover they were not called because of their intrinsic wisdom. In truth, we all have made mistakes. Hopefully, we have at least learned from them and developed humility because of them. This faultfinding demon, however, takes our past mistakes and parades them before our memory, criticizing our efforts to do God's will, thus keeping us in bondage to the past.

When the enemy pits us against one another, it first provokes us to jealousy or fear. The security of our place in life seems threatened by another's success. Perhaps to justify our personal failures or flaws, we magnify the past shortcomings of others. The more our jealousy grows, the more this demon exploits our thoughts until nothing about the individual or his church seems right.

In the final stage we actually wage a campaign against him. No defense he offers will satisfy us. We are convinced he is deceived and dangerous; we think it is up to us to warn others. Yet the truth is, the person whose mind is controlled by the fault-finder demon is the one who is deceived and dangerous. For his own unrepentant thoughts toward jealousy and fleshly criticism have supplied hell with a "lumberyard" of material to erect walls between members of the body of Christ.

Sadly, it is often leaders who have fallen from the intensity of their first love, who become the fiercest persecutors of others who are moving in the Holy Spirit. Christ's disciples will be persecuted, but this author can find no biblical authorization for Christians to persecute others. Persecution is a deed of the flesh. "But as at that time he who was born according to the flesh persecuted him who was born according to the Spirit, so it is now also" (Gal 4:29). Incredibly, those who are given to persecuting others often actually think that they are "offering service to God" (John 16:2).

To combat this enemy we must create an atmosphere of grace among us as individuals and between us as churches. Like the Father who has given us life, we must seek to cause all things to work together for good. If one stumbles, without condoning hypocrisy, we must be quick to cover him, for we are "members of one another" (Eph 4:25). As it is written, "None of you shall approach any blood relative of his to uncover nakedness; I am the Lord" (Lev 18:6). We are family, begotten from one Father. "Their nakedness you shall not uncover; for their nakedness is yours" (v 10). Even under the Old Covenant, it was unlawful to uncover another's mistake publicly. Love finds a redemptive way to cover a multitude of sins.

Where the Vultures Are Gathered

The accuser uses yet another weapon, and it uses this weapon astutely. There are times in our walk with God when, to increase fruitfulness, the Father prunes us back (see John 15). This is a season of preparation, where the Lord's purpose is to lead His servants into new power in ministry.

This growth process requires new levels of surrender as well as a fresh crucifixion of the flesh. It is often a time of humiliation and testing, of emptiness and seeming ineffectiveness as God expands our dependency upon Him. It can be a fearful time when our need is exposed in stark visibility.

Unfortunately, this time of weakness is apparent not only to the man or woman of God; it frequently occurs before the church, and before principalities and powers as well. The faultfinder spirit, and those who have come to think as it thinks, find in their target's vulnerability an opportunity to crush him.

Time and again, what would otherwise have become an incubator of life becomes a coffin of death. Those who might otherwise emerge with the clarity and power of prophetic vision are beaten down and abandoned, cut off from the very people who should have prayed them through to resurrection. In this attack the faultfinder is most destructive. For here this demon aborts the birth of mature ministries, those who would arm their churches for war.

The faultfinders and gossips are already planted in the church—perhaps you are such a one! When the living God is making your pastor more deeply dependent, and thus more easily shaped for His purposes, do you criticize his apparent lack of anointing? Although he did not abandon you during your time of need, do you abandon him now, when your faith might be the very encouragement he needs to fully yield to the cross?

Those who are sympathetic to the accuser of the brethren fulfill, by application, Matthew 24:28, "Wherever the corpse is, there the vultures will gather." The backbiting of these vulture-like individuals actually feeds their lower nature, for they seek what is dead in a church; they are attracted to what is dying.

Eventually these faultfinders depart, instinctively looking to take issue with some other church. "These are grumblers, finding fault . . . the ones who cause divisions" (Jude 16–19). They leave behind their former brethren severely wounded and in strife, and a pastor greatly disheartened. Soon they join a new church and, in time, God begins to deal with this new pastor. Once again the faultfinder spirit manifests itself through them, strategically positioned to destroy another church.

Today, God is seeking to raise up His servants with increased power and authority. In the pruning stage of their growth, will we water their dryness with prayer or will we be vultures drawn to devour their dying flesh?

How to Correct Error

When the accuser comes, it brings distorted facts and condemnation. Those who are trapped by this spirit never research the virtues in the organization or person they are attacking.

With the same zeal that the faultfinders seek to unearth sin, those who will conquer this enemy must earnestly seek God's heart and His calling for those they would reprove.

True correction, therefore, will proceed with reverence, not revenge. Indeed, are not those whom we seek to correct Christ's servants? Are they not His possession? Is it possible the works of which we are jealous, and thus critical, might be the very works of Christ? Also, let us ask ourselves: why has God chosen us to bring His rebuke? Are we walking in Christ's pattern?

These are important questions, for to be anointed with Christ's authority to rebuke, we must be committed to men with Christ's love. But, if we are angry, embittered or jealous toward another we cannot even pray correctly for that person, much less reprove him. Jesus, the great Lion of Judah, was declared worthy to bring forth judgment by virtue of His nature: He was a Lamb slain for men's sin. If we are not determined to die for men, we have no right to judge them.

Those who seek to justify leaving a church must not do so simply through finding fault. Rather, we should openly communicate with the ministerial team. Our attitude should be one of prayer and love, leaving a blessing for what we gained by our time spent in the church. If there has indeed been sin in the ministry, we should contact the church authorities in the city and leave the situation with them.

Additionally, local ministers should be in communication with one another, never basing their opinion of another church or leader on the testimony of one who has just left it. If people join your congregation and bring with them a root of bitterness against their former assembly, that root will spring up in your church and many will be defiled. Therefore, no matter how much you need "new members," never build your congregation with individuals who are unreconciled to their former fellowship.

Indeed, the Lord's word to us is that in the house of the Lord criticism must be replaced with prayer, and faultfinding eliminated with a covering love. Where there is error, we must go with a motive to restore. Where there are wrong doctrines, let us maintain a gentle spirit, correcting those in opposition.

Let's pray: *Lord Jesus, forgive us for our lack of prayer and the weakness of our love. Master, we want to be like You, that when we see a need, instead of criticizing, we lay down our lives for it. Lord, heal Your church of this demonic stronghold! In Jesus' name. Amen.*

—FROM THE BOOK, THE HOUSE OF THE LORD

SELF TEST, CHAPTER SIX

Remember, we are looking for answers that correspond with this training. Please write out your essay answers, allowing the Holy Spirit to provoke your thoughts. You may want to use them for group discussion. Note: we do not provide answers to essay questions. To check your multiple choice answers, see answer key in the next session.

Chapter 6, Essay #1: Are you now better able to see how Satan has been the accuser of the brethren during times of strife?

Chapter 6, Essay #2: In what ways can you walk in a deeper commitment to replacing criticism with prayer and faultfinding with love?

1. In exposing the activity of the accuser of the brethren, our goal is to see the living church _____ and to have

   _____.
   a. no longer broadcast in the media; less immorality
   b. delivered from the stronghold of faultfinding; our hearts turned to prayer
   c. separated from the state; less need for prayer or healing
   d. exempt from judgment; increased manifestations

2. What is the intent of Satan's assault of faultfinding demons against the body of Christ?
   a. to hinder the next move of God
   b. to entice us away from the perfections of Jesus
   c. to get us to focus on the imperfections of one another
   d. all the above

3. When we see things wrong or lacking, or imperfections in others, the measure of our Christlike maturity is revealed in:
   a. what we do with what we see
   b. the accuracy of our confrontation
   c. knowing or discerning without needing to consult or listen to the individual
   d. all the above

4. The timing of the accuser of the brethren's attack is almost always:
   a. discerned by the congregation
   b. when we are not working toward advancing God's kingdom
   c. both a & d
   d. just prior to, or immediately after, a significant breakthrough

5. When the accuser seduces individuals, nearly all involved _____, ignoring that Jesus is praying for His body to become one.
   a. become lethargic
   b. take their eyes off Jesus and focus upon "issues"
   c. lay down their defensiveness
   d. become intently focused on the "true" issues

6. Christ's pattern of bringing correction:
   a. offering grace for change
   b. giving time to repent
   c. sandwiching rebuke between encouragement, praise and promises
   d. all the above

7. What weapons can we expose that the accuser uses against us?
   a. our actual sins, and failure to repent; past mistakes and poor decisions
   b. the virtues and values God has formed in us
   c. our vulnerability in times of weakness or seasons of preparation, when God is pruning us
   d. both a & c

8. How can we disarm the accuser's weapons?
   a. create an atmosphere of grace among and between us, with love redemptively covering over a multitude of sins
   b. repent when the Holy Spirit desires to correct us
   c. pray for one another instead of preying on one another
   d. all the above

> **QUOTE:**
>
> *"What we do with what we see, however, is the measure of Christlike maturity. Remember, when Jesus saw the condition of mankind, He 'emptied Himself, taking the form of a bond-servant . . . He humbled Himself by becoming obedient to the point of death, even death on a cross' (Phil 2:7–8). He died to take away sin, He did not just judge them."*

CHAPTER SEVEN

INTERCESSION, JEZEBEL AND SPIRITUAL AUTHORITY

JEZEBEL'S WAR AGAINST SPIRITUAL AUTHORITY

The spirit of Jezebel will target, and then seek to divide, the relationship between a pastor and the church intercessors. The antidote? Let the senior leader appreciate, communicate and support his intercessors and esteem their contribution, and let the intercessors set their prayer focus to first seek the spiritual fulfillment of the senior pastor's vision.

Pastoral leaders are under siege. At every conference where I speak, various pastors approach and tell of terrible experiences with Jezebel-like battles in their churches. But I don't have to travel to be informed, for not a week passes where I do not hear from pastors from many places via phone, letters or e-mails—each desperate for specific prayer concerning the conflict in their churches. The war is over one thing: Satan seeks to neutralize spiritual authority, and no enemy of hell does this more efficiently than the spirit of Jezebel.

When the Jezebel spirit attacks the church leadership—whether it involves temptation, confusion, witchcraft, fear or discouragement—it will always have as its ultimate purpose to disable the spiritual authority of pastoral leadership. Thus, Jesus promised that the church that overcomes Jezebel will be granted "authority over the nations" (see Rev 2:26–28). The Jezebel spirit seeks to divide, diminish and then displace the spiritual authority God has given church leaders.

Without pastors leading in godly authority, a church simply cannot function: confusion, ambition and chaos reign. True spiritual authority is a source of protection; it is a living shelter that covers and nurtures a home or church. Satan seeks to neutralize the leader in that Christian setting, for if he can strike the shepherd, he can scatter the sheep.

One way in which the Jezebel spirit attacks churches is by dividing intercessors from pastoral authority. We need intercessors, for without them we literally would not move forward. However, when an intercessor assumes that their "prophetic witness" is the guiding light of the church, or when they stand apart from the church leader and offer a different vision than what the leadership presents, it is actually Jezebel infiltrating that church to bring division.

The deception deepens, for often those who present a vision different than the pastoral leaders' vision are presenting something that could seem godly. It is the spirit or attitude through which they communicate their perceptions that opens the door to Jezebel. The unbending demand that a leader conform to both their prophetic witness and the timing of its implementation is where this spirit gains access and causes division.

PRAY THE SENIOR LEADER'S VISION

The best relationship between a pastor and the church intercessors occurs when intercessors simply pray the vision of the senior church leader. His responsibility is to lead; their responsibility is to intercede. They are not called to try to make their church become like some other church. For to do so becomes a great source of strife and heartache for all.

God has a unique call, or responsibility, that He bestows upon every congregation. That sense of direction and purpose for the local church is usually given to its founding pastor. When he leaves, the vision of the church is passed on to the church elders who, in turn, look for a new pastor who can build upon God's historic call to that congregation.

The senior leader of a church, though certainly imperfect, is still appointed by God as the "head of the house" (see Matt 24:43). This senior pastor, working together with his associate leaders, has the responsibility to incorporate into the church structure what the Lord brings to him. This responsibility presents itself through a variety of sources. His "leading" may come personally from the Lord, or it might emerge from counsel with his elders or other peers; it might arise from inspiration from various authors or information gained from conference speakers and other pastors. Not the least of his resources in finding God's heart would be the intercessors in the church. But intercessors must accept that the responsibility to guide the congregational household comes from God to a leader, not to the intercessors. As imperfect as that leader may be, intercessors must learn to not introduce a different vision than that which is currently guiding the congregation through the senior leader.

When one or more intercessors seek to manipulate, pressure or control the church leader with a prophetic witness, beware: the Jezebel spirit is at work. When church members are being disconnected from the senior leader through a whispering campaign and are now following a "prophetic witness," beware: again, the tactic comes from Jezebel. Remember, Jesus said of Jezebel, "She calls herself a prophetess." Beware of self-appointed spiritual authorities in the church that undermine the authority of the senior leader or leadership team.

Instead of following the trail of the discontented prophetic whisperer, pray the vision of the senior pastor. If he does not have a vision, ask him to write one up so you can support his vision and help see it fulfilled. When you have a witness borne of prayer, submit it to the senior leader in meekness and let him (or him and his associate ministry team) discern it. But do not be offended if the timing of implementation comes much later or even not at all. Perhaps the word you sensed was not for everyone, but for you.

GOD LOVES ORDER

One cannot truly know God nor appreciate Him as He is without being awed at the ordered array of His universe. Yes, the Almighty loves life and freedom, but at the substructure of all creation there first had to exist an immutable matrix of order. It was upon this foundation of ordered laws of physics that life emerged. Order is the source of life.

We must remember that the very same eternal mind that created the structured order of the universe created the church. There is a divine order to the church that begins in being rightly related to Christ and the leadership He gives to the church through people. God is a God of order; order precedes life and freedom. God's mind is ordered; His will is ordered and He gives "orders" to put things in order.

It is important to note that the Lord Himself honors the order He creates. Consider: the Lord appeared to Paul, spoke to him, actually blinded him in His glory, and then said, "Rise, and enter the city, and it shall be told you what you must do" (Acts 9:6). Why didn't the Lord just heal Paul? Why didn't He just tell Paul what he had to do? Paul would have to learn that, to reach God, he would have to submit to man. This is God's order and the Lord Himself honored it. Paul had to hear about Jesus from Ananias.

Or consider Cornelius: an angel appeared to this Roman centurion in a dream and told him that a man named Simon Peter would explain to him the way of salvation. Why didn't the angel simply tell Cornelius about Jesus? In the Almighty's universe, God works in an ordered fashion. Before the Gentiles could enter the kingdom en masse they would be invited by the Jews, who first accepted Christ. God honored the order He created.

Consider church protocol in the book of Acts. When Philip brought the gospel to Samaria after Pentecost, miracles, conversions and great signs were accomplished. But Philip would not lay his hands upon the Samaritans to receive the Holy Spirit. Why? Because until this time, the Holy Spirit had only spread through the hands of the first apostles. Again, God required His servant to respect the order and authority of the first apostles.

God has an order in your church. However it is established, and in whatever way it is defined, it is a place in order and it should be respected and honored. It does not matter whether you agree or not with the governmental structure within a church; as long as you attend that fellowship you should honor the order. Most congregations are led by a pastor; in some, the authority resides in the elder or deacon board; in still others, the authority comes from a bishop or even a prophetic or apostolic ministry. Whatever the structure, honor it and submit to it without dissension. If you feel you cannot grow in that congregation under its present structure, find a church where you can develop spiritually. However, do not cause strife just because you are not familiar or comfortable with the order.

The issue is not the form of government, but the life within the form. Paul wrote of apostles and prophets, evangelists, pastors and teachers; John, however, spoke of the church in terms of fathers, young men and children; Peter, on the other hand, taught of elders, shepherds and the flock of God. The issue is not how the order is defined, but to understand that there is an order already established in a church and that order should be honored. It can be changed, but to change a church structure, one must submit to the elders of that church and be in agreement with the senior leader. They will pay the price for change when they are convinced God is leading. But they should not be forced to change just because someone has a problem with a church expression.

When the Jezebel spirit begins to manifest in a church, it immediately seeks to undermine the authority structure. If it cannot directly seduce a leader or cause him to commit immorality (and use that sin to diminish his authority), it will bring strife and division to challenge his authority in the church. Bear in mind that the spirit which produced Jezebel existed before its namesake was born. Although we refer to Jezebel as "she," this spirit is without gender. However, it is important to note that, while men in leadership are the main target of most principalities, Jezebel is more attracted to the uniqueness of the female psyche in its sophisticated ability to manipulate without physical force. Remember, Jezebel was a queen who ruled a king; she assumes a "prophetess" role so she can rule a church. In so doing, she seeks to create a counterfeit authority among groups of individuals in a congregation. The result is that the established order in the church is undermined, true authority is neutralized, and leaders are wearied by endless meetings.

> And angels who did not keep their own domain, but abandoned their proper abode, He has kept in eternal bonds under darkness for the judgment of the great day.   —Jude 1:6

There is a proper abode for each of us in the order of God. Jesus said that in the Father's house there were "many dwelling places" and that He was going to prepare a place for each of us. The Father's house is not only a place found in heaven; it is revealed here on earth in the body of Christ. Whenever we seek to break the order of our church, we leave our proper place and enter a realm "kept in eternal bonds under darkness."

My friends, stay loyal to the church order where you worship God. If that order does not fit your temperament, find a church that does. If you cannot find a church, perhaps you are called to start one where your vision of Christianity can be fulfilled. But whatever you do, do not open up to false authority; do not dishonor the authority in your local fellowship through gossip or dissension; rather pray the vision of the senior pastor. For in so doing, you will help bring the church into the destiny of God and serve to fulfill the uniqueness of God's purpose.

Let's pray: *Thank You, God, for establishing order on this earth and in Your church. I realize that my pastor is not perfect, but neither am I. Help me to work together with You and serve the vision of my pastor as we all become more Christlike in the process.*

FROM THE *ICIT* WEEKLY MAILER

SELF TEST, CHAPTER SEVEN

Remember, we are looking for answers that correspond with this training. Please write out your essay answers, allowing the Holy Spirit to provoke your thoughts. You may want to use them for group discussion. Note: we do not provide answers to essay questions. To check your multiple choice answers, see answer key in the next session.

#1.
I Believe God
has an order for us
all things, all of us
are blessed, gifted,
most pastor have the
gift of church leadership
Therefore I have faith
to attend under that
leadership. to not
I have the option to not
attend elsewhere

 # 2. yes. i follow
Jesus says to follow
Him.

Chapter 7, Essay #1: Share your insights regarding God's order in the church.

Chapter 7, Essay #2: Are you willing to pray for your leaders, covering them through your submission to the authority God has given them?

1. When the spirit of Jezebel attacks a church, what is its ultimate purpose?
    a. to divide the relationship between a pastor and the church intercessors
    b. to disable spiritual authority of pastoral leadership
    c. to bring new vision and revelation to the pastoral leadership
    d. both a & b

2. How could an intercessor with a prophetic witness actually open the door to Jezebel?
    a. by assuming their witness is the guiding light of the church
    b. standing apart from the church leader, offering a different vision
    c. by the spirit or attitude through which they communicate their perceptions
    d. all the above

3. Generally speaking, what is the church intercessor's primary responsibility in relationship to their local church?
    a. guiding the congregational household
    b. to move church leadership toward new vision
    c. pray the vision of the senior church leader
    d. none of the above

4. Jesus said of Jezebel, "She calls herself a prophetess." What would this spirit look like in the church?
    a. self-appointed spiritual authority that undermines the authority of the senior leader or leadership team
    b. like a sneaky person
    c. one who is never involved in church leadership
    d. all the above

5. When you have a witness borne in prayer, what should you do with it?
    a. share it with others in the congregation first
    b. submit it to the senior leader, then do not be offended if timing of implementation comes much later or even not at all

c. tell the leadership when you are absolutely sure, and don't back down from the vision God has given you

d. nothing at all

6. In what way did the Lord Himself honor His order when He appeared to Paul?

   a. by leaving Paul to hear from Ananias to learn that, in certain vital truths, to reach God, he would have to submit to man

   b. by telling Paul about Himself, and exactly what to do

   c. by immediately healing Paul

   d. all the above

7. What should you do if you disagree with the governmental structure within a church you are attending?

   a. use Scripture to point out correct form of government

   b. keep attending but don't participate in the things you disagree with

   c. honor the order that is established there

   d. try to bring positive change

8. How does the Jezebel spirit seek to undermine the authority structure or established order in a church?

   a. by tempting a leader to sin and using that sin to diminish his authority

   b. by creating a counterfeit authority among groups, disconnecting members from the leader

   c. by encouraging repentance

   d. both a & b

> **QUOTE:**
>
> *"God is a God of order; order precedes life and freedom. God's mind is ordered; His will is ordered and He gives 'orders' to put things in order."*

Session Five:

Prayer in Pursuit of God's Presence

CHAPTER EIGHT

UNRELENTING LOVE

The Bible describes our relationship with Christ in strong, symbolic pictures of oneness: He is head of a body, husband of a wife, God in His temple. In spite of these powerful metaphors, a sense of distance remains between the Presence of the Lord and us. This distance is a test. Our call is to possess that love of God which reaches into eternity and brings the glory and Person of Christ into His earthly house.

THOSE WHO SEEK AFTER GOD

"God has looked down from heaven upon the sons of men, to see if there is anyone who understands, who seeks after God" (Ps 53:2). We simply must have more of Jesus. In the face of increasing wickedness in the world, our programs and ideas have failed. We need God. Those who understand the hour we face are seeking Him. The wise know that Christ Himself is our only strategy and hope. If just one soul in a city truly attains the hope of this chapter, that individual will change his or her world.

This message is about seeking the Lord. Our text will be from the Song of Solomon 3:1–4, for here we find a bride and bridegroom who both are intolerant of the distance between them. The bride in the passage symbolizes the church in her deepest longings for Jesus; the bridegroom symbolizes Christ. We will start with verse one; the bride is speaking.

"On my bed night after night I sought him whom my soul loves." True seeking of God is born out of love. Our quest for God is not a matter of discipline but of desire. It is not a question of sacrifice but of undistracted love. Your sleep is gone because your beloved is gone. You *must* seek Him, for such is the nature of love.

Some will say, "But I already know the Lord. I have found Him." In truth, it was He who found us. Our salvation rests securely upon this fact. But while many are resting upon Christ's finding us, His bride arises now to find Him. In the very love which He inspired, she pursues her beloved.

We must see that there is still much more to learn and discover about our Lord. At the end of Moses' life, after being used by God to confront and defeat the gods of Egypt, after dwelling in the Lord's glory for forty years, he prays, "Thou hast *begun* to show Thy servant Thy greatness and Thy strong hand" (Deut 3:24). For all we think we know, we have seen but a glimpse of His glory. The apostle Paul wrote, "As many as are perfect, have this attitude" (Phil 3:15). To seek and know Christ is the attitude of the mature; it is the singular obsession of Christ's bride.

In this maturation process, there will come a point when, within your heart, love for God will take ascendancy over mere intellectual or doctrinal understanding. The bride of Christ cannot contain her longing nor patronize her aching heart by saying, "I will feel better in the morning." There is simply no reconciling the passion of her soul with the absence of her beloved.

Note also there is an unfolding dimension to seeking the Lord which we must embrace. *Genuine love for God is an unrelenting hunger.* As you would die without food, so you feel you will die without Him. She says, "Night after night I sought him." The knowledge of what her beloved has done in the past, a "religion" about Him, will provide little solace for the bride. She wants Him!

Overcoming Resistance

There are many obstacles which hinder us from truly finding the Lord. The bride mourns, "I sought him whom my soul loves. I sought him but did not find him." Her first attempts at seeking her beloved prove fruitless, yet, unlike most of us, she does not terminate her quest. Augustine said it well: "God is not on the surface." There is, indeed, a "secret place of the Most High." Although hidden, it is accessible.

Another deterrent is the "effects" of drawing near to the Lord: the blessings of encouragement or a new understanding of Scripture. We must guard against these signposts becoming our final destination. We must not be deterred by goose bumps or tears, edification or comfort. We are searching for Jesus Himself.

Let us also understand, we will not find His fullness by seeking Him merely in convenient times and comfortable places. Rather, our quest is a determined, continual pilgrimage which will not end until He is disclosed to us (see Phil 3:12). We are confident, though, for He has promised that, in the day we seek Him with our whole hearts, we shall find Him (see Jer 29:13).

Christ Our Life

For many, Christianity is simply the religion into which they were born. For others, although Jesus is truly their Savior, their relationship with Him is hardly more that a history lesson, a study of what He did in the past. For those who attain His Presence, however, Christ is Savior and more: He is their very life (see Col 3:4). When Jesus is your life, you cannot go on without Him.

There is a story of a man who, in search of God, came to study at the feet of an old teacher. The sage brought this young man to a lake and led him out into the shoulder-deep water. Putting his hands upon his pupil's head, he promptly pushed him under the water and held him there until the disciple, feeling he would surely drown, frantically repelled the old man's resistance. In shock and confusion the young man resurfaced. "What is the meaning of this?" he demanded. His teacher looked him in the eyes and said, "When you desire God as you desired air, you shall find Him."

Was this not the attitude of the psalmist when he wrote, "As the deer pants for the water brooks, so my soul pants for Thee, O God" (Ps 42:1)? The question here is not only of desire, but of survival. I need Him as a drowning man needs air and as a parched deer needs water. How can I exist without abiding in the living Christ?

The bride continues, "I must arise now and go about the city; in the streets and in the squares I must seek him whom my soul loves." This inexorable woman has risen from the security of her own bed. She has left the comfort of her warm house and now is seeking her beloved in the streets and in the squares. Pastors, be aware: Not all who wander from church to church are uncommitted or superficial Christians. A significant number are honestly searching for Christ. They are asking, "Have you seen Him?"

Not only is the bride in the streets and squares of Christianity; she is facing the force and the power of darkness as well. Yet nothing stops her—not her own need of sleep nor her fear of the night. The love of Christ compels her.

However, again she is disappointed. "I sought him but did not find him." We might think that after so great an effort—and in the face of the seeming reluctance of heaven to answer her cry—

she would feel justified to return home. But she does not. We too must guard against becoming satisfied with our opinion of ourselves: "We prayed; we waited; we searched for God. We did more than other men." This false reward fills the soul with self-exaltation. If we would truly find Him, we must stay empty and hungry for God alone.

"The watchmen who make the rounds in the city found me, and I said, 'Have you seen him whom my soul loves?'" From her bed to the streets and now to the watchmen, the bride is seeking her lover. Notice that the watchmen found *her.* The watchmen are the modern-day prophetic ministries. Their highest calling is to find the searching bride and direct her to Jesus. While many may come to the seers for a word of encouragement or revelation, the bride is looking for Jesus. Her singleness of purpose is undistracted; she asks the watchmen, "Have you seen Him?"

"Scarcely had I left them when I found him whom my soul loves." This is the greatest motivation for seeking the Lord: The time will come when you find Him! You will pass your tests and overcome the obstacles; you will be secure in the embrace of Christ.

She says, "I held on to him and would not let him go." I am reminded of Mary at the empty tomb of Christ. The apostles came, looked in the cave and went away astounded. But Mary came to the tomb and lingered, weeping. The death of Christ was horrible, but the empty tomb was unbearable. She had to find Him whom her soul loved!

The Scripture says that Jesus Himself came to her, but in her sorrow she did not recognize Him. He said, "Woman, why are you weeping? Whom are you seeking?" Can we see the connection here between Mary's weeping and her seeking Christ? Blinded by her tears, she supposes He is the gardener. "Sir, if you have carried Him away, tell me where you have laid Him, and I will take Him away."

"Jesus said to her, 'Mary!' She turned and said to Him in Hebrew, 'Rabboni!' (which means, Teacher). Jesus said to her, 'Stop clinging to Me, for I have not yet ascended to the Father' " (John 20:15–17).

The instant Mary sees the Lord she clings to Him. And here is the most astounding event, indeed, the marvel of all marvels: Jesus said, "I have not yet ascended." *Christ interrupted His ascent into heaven to answer this woman's love!* In the very process of His resurrection, He is drawn—No! compelled—toward her weeping! Jesus demonstrated that love is the highest, most powerful law of His kingdom!

When you expend your energies, your nights, your heart; when you overcome your fears out of love for Jesus, you will find Him and "never let him go." Mary found Him whom her soul loved. She continued in her pursuit, remaining in sorrow until she found Him. The disciples had gone home. To whom did Jesus appear first? He came to the one who had the highest passion for Him. And she clung to Him.

BRINGING JESUS TO OUR MOTHER'S HOUSE

"I found him whom my soul loves; I held on to him and would not let him go, until I had brought him to my mother's house, and into the room of her who conceived me." You have laid hold of Jesus; you have found fulfillment. Yet, has this seeking of God been only for you? No. For the bride brings Him to the house of her mother, which is the church. She brings Him back to the needy and hurting, to her brothers and her sisters.

We all want the Lord, but only the bride will go so far as to find Him and bring Him back to the house. I want to charge you to find Jesus. Do not merely talk about how dead your life or church is—find Him! Pass through your fears. Overcome your passivity and lay hold of Him. The church, even our cities, need people who are anointed with the Presence of Jesus!

You Have Made His Heart Beat Faster

Where was Jesus throughout the time of the bride searching? Was He aloof, indifferent, sitting in heaven? From the beginning He had been watching, actually longing, for His bride to find Him. He now speaks: "You have made my heart beat faster, my sister, my bride; you have made my heart beat faster with a single glance of your eyes" (Song 4:9).

Listen to me: *You are His bride. He is returning from heaven for you!* The single glance of your eyes toward Him makes His heart beat faster. Such love is inconceivable. He sees your repentance as your preparation for Him—His bride making herself ready. He beholds you kneeling, weeping at your bedside. He shares your painful longing. He has been watching. And the bridegroom says, "The glance of your eyes has made my heart beat faster."

The Lord has a promise for His bride. He said there will be a fresh and overwhelming baptism of love that will surpass all our knowledge of Him. We would know the height and depth, the width and the breadth of His love. While yet here on earth, we will be filled with His fullness.

We have many tasks, even responsibilities, which have come from heaven. However, the need of our soul is to be with Jesus. The areas of sin in our lives exist simply because we have lived too far from Him. Let us commit our hearts to seeking our God. Let us find Him whom our soul loves and bring Him back to the house of the Lord!

"[That you may really come] to know—practically, through experience for yourselves—the love of Christ, which far surpasses mere knowledge (without experience); that you may be filled (through all your being) unto all the fullness of God—[that is] may have the richest measure of the divine Presence, and become a body wholly filled and flooded with God Himself!" (Eph 3:19 AMPLIFIED)

Let's pray: *Lord, even now I lift my eyes toward You. Jesus, Your Word says that even the glance of my eyes makes Your heart beat faster. Lord, I am dark with sin, yet I choose to respond to the initiative of Your love. I put on the wedding garments You have purchased for me. Baptize me afresh in the passion of Your love until I am consumed with even the thought of You.*

—FROM THE BOOK, *THE HOUSE OF THE LORD*

SELF TEST, CHAPTER EIGHT

Remember, we are looking for answers that correspond with this training. Please write out your essay answers, allowing the Holy Spirit to provoke your thoughts. You may want to use them for group discussion. Note: we do not provide answers to essay questions. To check your multiple choice answers, see answer key in the next session.

Chapter 8, Essay #1: Have you had moments when you have overcome your fears and found Jesus, and never wanted to let Him go?

Chapter 8, Essay #2: If the need of our soul is to be with Jesus, then how can we move closer to Him?

1. True God-seeking is born out of:
   a. sacrifice
   b. discipline
   c. undistracted love
   d. rest

2. What is the singular obsession of Christ's bride and the attitude of the mature?
   a. to seek an up-front ministry
   b. to seek and know Jesus Christ
   c. to confront that which needs to change
   d. to keep everyone going in the same direction

3. There is an unfolding dimension to seeking the Lord which we must embrace. Genuine love for God is:
   a. an unrelenting hunger
   b. as you would die for food, so you feel you will die without Him
   c. the knowledge of a "religion" about Him that provides solace for seeking Him
   d. both a & b

4. What obstacles hinder us from truly finding the Lord?
   a. when attempts seem fruitless and we terminate our quest to find Him
   b. the boulders we stumble over
   c. when the "effects" of drawing near to the Lord become our final destination
   d. both a & c

5. How do we find His fullness?
   a. by seeking Him when it's most convenient
   b. by seeking Him in ways we are most comfortable
   c. when we seek Him with our whole heart
   d. by looking for signs of encouragement or revelation and stopping there

6. What was the attitude and meaning of the psalmist when he wrote, "As the deer pants for the water brooks, so my soul pants for Thee, O God" (Ps 42:1)?
   a. We get exhausted seeking after Him and can feel justified to stop seeking.
   b. We can exist as long as we have water.
   c. Needing God is a matter of survival just as the deer needed water.
   d. all the above

7. After Jesus rose from the dead, to whom did He appear first?
   a. the one who had the highest passion for Him
   b. the disciples
   c. Mary
   d. both a & c

8. The true bride will find Jesus and then _____.
   a. bring Him back to the church
   b. retreat to her own place
   c. will relent in her love for Him
   d. all the above

> **QUOTE:**
>
> *"Let us also understand, we will not find His fullness by seeking Him merely in convenient times and comfortable places. Rather, our quest is a determined, continual pilgrimage which will not end until He is disclosed to us (see Phil 3:12). We are confident, though, for He has promised that, in the day we seek Him with our whole hearts, we shall find Him (see Jer 29:13)"*

CHAPTER NINE

"TELL FRANCIS I MISS HIM"

If all these things are true and the glory of the Lord is going to increase, what shall we do in preparation?

We cannot attain the glory that is coming if we do not esteem the glory that is here now. At this very moment, the Presence of the Lord is accessible to each of us. Yet, to *enter* His Presence and abide with Him is God's goal for us. It is also the very thing Satan fights against the hardest.

The nature of this battle is not easily discerned. The enemy does not appear with fierce countenance; He does not threaten us with retaliation if we begin to seek God. Satan is far more subtle. He manipulates the *good* things of God's blessings to keep us from the best gift: God's Presence.

The devil has a willing accomplice in our fleshly nature. Solomon noted, "Behold, I have found only this, that God made men upright, but they have sought out many devices" (Eccl 7:29). Our "many devices," gadgets, and technologies, for all the convenience they provide, will not sustain us in the days ahead. *There simply will be no substitute for God.* Instead of having hearts full of God, we are full of desires for the things of this life.

Remember, Jesus warned:

Be on guard, that your hearts may not be weighted down with dissipation and drunkenness and the worries of life, and that day come on you suddenly like a trap; for it will come upon all those who dwell on the face of all the earth.   —Luke 21:34–35

Too many Christians are simply dissipated and drained by the attractions and surpluses of our prosperous society. Let me assure you, most of these things are not evil in themselves, especially when accommodated in moderation. The deception is in our definition of moderation, for what seems like a modest lifestyle to us would be excess and luxury to ninety percent of the world.

Pursuing the pleasures of this world can become intoxicating. It is here where Satan's activity is most veiled. Instead of seeking God and being available for His will, many of us are entangled in debt and desire. Like the ancient Babylonians, ours is a "land of images, and [we] are mad over idols" (Jer 50:38 AMPLIFIED). Many Christians are caught in a maze of distractions.

Idolatry is so familiar to us, we think it not strange! We actually call our sports and movie stars "idols." These individuals are, in turn, *idolized* by millions of followers. Yet, whatever we continually idolize eventually will demonize our lives.

It is in the midst of this great societal prosperity and a multitude of distractions that the Lord wants us to walk with a single mind toward His glory. Can we do it? Yes, but we may need to rid ourselves of our televisions, or at least fast from them for a month. If that is too much, deny it entrance into your mind for a week. The degree of difficulty in turning the television off is the measure of our bondage. If we cannot let it go, it is because we are its captive.

In a land where excess, ambition, and envy are the counselors of men, only those who abide in the simplicity of Christ are truly free. We must choose to make our portion in life the Presence of God.

Jesus said, "Blessed are the poor in spirit, for theirs is the kingdom of heaven" (Matt 5:3). To be poor in spirit is to be free of hidden greed; it is to see and possess the kingdom of heaven.

If you are truly liberated from greed—if, indeed, you do not bow to mammon—God will begin to release His wealth to you. If your heart truly becomes the Lord's possession, He will begin to entrust to you His possessions, both heavenly and earthly. As you become Christ's slave, the earth will be your slave; it, too, will yield its resources for the purposes of God.

WEARINESS IN WELL-DOING

If Satan cannot distract you with worldliness, he will seek to wear you out, even using the good works you are doing for the Lord as a means of draining your energy. In fact, Daniel speaks of a time at the end of the age when the enemy will attempt to "wear down the saints of the Highest One" (Dan 7:25).

God never intended for us to do His will without His Presence. The power to accomplish God's purpose comes from prayer and intimacy with Christ. It is here, closed in with God, where we find an ever-replenishing flow of spiritual virtue.

In the beginning of my ministry, the Lord called me to consecrate to Him the time from dawn until noon. I spent these hours in prayer, worship, and the study of His Word. I would often worship God for hours, writing songs to Him that came from this wonderful sanctuary of love. The Presence of the Lord was my delight, and I know my time with Him was not only well-spent but well-pleasing to us both.

However, as my life began to bear the fruit of Christ's influence, the Holy Spirit would bring people to me for ministry. In time, as more people would come, I found myself cutting off forty-five minutes from the end of my devotional time. Ministry would extend into the night, and I stopped rising as early as I had.

Church growth problems began to eat at the quality of my remaining time; ministerial expansion, training younger ministries, and more counseling and deliverance crowded the already limited time I had left. Of course, these changes did not happen overnight, but the months and years of increasing success were steadily eroding my devotional life. In time I found myself in a growing ministry but with a shrinking anointing to sustain it.

One day an intercessor called who prayed regularly for me. He told me that during the night the Lord spoke to him in a dream concerning me. I was eager to hear what the Lord had spoken to my friend, thinking perhaps He was going to increase our outreach or maybe supply some needed finances. I asked Him to tell me the dream.

What the Lord said had nothing to do with the things that were consuming my time. He simply said, *"Tell Francis I miss him."*

Oh, what burdens we carry—what weariness accumulates—when we neglect the privilege of daily spending time with Jesus. I cried as I repented before the Lord, and I readjusted my priorities. No longer would I counsel people in the mornings. I would spend this time again with God.

Yet, I thought I might lose some of the people who had recently joined the church. These were people who had come specifically for personal ministry. I knew I would not have the same time for them as before, but I had to make my decision for God.

The next Sunday morning I announced to the congregation that my mornings were off limits, consecrated to God. "Please," I said, "no calls or counseling. I need to spend time with Christ." What happened next shocked me. The entire church rose and applauded! It seems they wanted a pastor who spent more time with God! They were tired of a tired pastor.

As we enter the days of His Presence, our primary activity will be to minister to Christ. Certainly there will be increased pressures. There will also be times of great harvest and spiritual activity. No matter what circumstances surround us, we must position ourselves first and continually in the Presence of God. For to miss our time with Jesus is to miss His glory in the day of His Presence.

Let's pray: *Dear Lord, oh, may I not get trapped in a maze of distractions. May all of the world's "timesaving devises" not rob me of my heavenly time with You.*

—FROM THE BOOK, *THE DAYS OF HIS PRESENCE*

#1. Spend the time with Him - Worship, pray, scripture - Serve

#2. Spiritual Death

SELF TEST, CHAPTER NINE

Remember, we are looking for answers that correspond with this training. Please write out your essay answers, allowing the Holy Spirit to provoke your thoughts. You may want to use them for group discussion. Note: we do not provide answers to essay questions. To check your multiple choice answers, see answer key in the next session.

Chapter 9, Essay #1: If the glory of the Lord is going to increase, what shall we do in preparation?

Chapter 9, Essay #2: Expand on the devastation we may experience when we let our devotional life erode.

1. What do we need to guard against that displaces having our hearts full of God?
    a. fasting
    b. desires for the things of this life
    c. too much worship
    d. all the above

2. Most of the things attracting us are not evil in themselves, especially when accommodated in moderation. The deception is in _____.
    a. our definition of moderation
    b. living in a prosperous society while walking singleminded toward His glory
    c. watching TV
    d. entertainment

3. What are Satan's subtle attempts to keep us from God's presence?
    a. distracts us with worldliness
    b. wears us out in good works
    c. rids us of our televisions
    d. both a & b

4. The power to accomplish God's purpose comes from:
    a. excellent ideas
    b. prayer and intimacy with Christ
    c. His presence
    d. both b & c

5. In a land where excess, ambition, and envy are the counselors of men, what must we choose to do in order to be liberated from greed?
    a. abide in the simplicity of Christ
    b. be poor in spirit and free of hidden greed, as in Matthew 5:3
    c. make our portion in life the Presence of God
    d. all the above

6. What is Daniel speaking of (in Daniel 7:25) about "wearing down the saints"?
    a. that we need to work less
    b. people in the church are hard workers
    c. a time at the end of the age when the enemy will seek to wear us out, using the good works we are doing for the Lord as a means of draining our energy
    d. that we need our rough edges worn down

7. What did Pastor Francis have to do to consecrate time with God?
   a. make a decision for God even over the good of time counseling people
   b. ignore the people who were calling and needing his time
   c. reprimand the congregation for distracting him
   d. spend his time with God after normal hours

8. What happened to Pastor Francis' time consecrated for the Lord when his life began to bear the fruit of Christ's influence and the Holy Spirit began bringing more opportunities for ministry?
   a. It stopped completely.
   b. His time with God gradually became crowded out, becoming less and less.
   c. It didn't affect his time with God.
   d. His time with God became easier to be set apart.

Session Six:

The Ultimate Vision;
The Most Powerful Prayer

SESSION SIX AUDIO MESSAGES:

6a. Awakening the Pleasure of God (part 1)
6b. Awakening the Pleasure of God (part 2)

ANSWER KEY TO LAST SESSION'S
SELF TEST QUESTIONS:

CHAPTER EIGHT. Unrelenting Love
1.c, 2.b, 3.d, 4.d, 5.c, 6.c, 7.d, 8.a.
CHAPTER NINE. "Tell Francis I Miss Him"
1.b, 2.a, 3.d, 4.d, 5.d, 6.c, 7.a, 8.b.

CHAPTER TEN

GOD TALKING TO GOD

Even one mercy-motivated intercessor has tremendous influence upon the heart of God. Consider Abraham's intercession for Sodom or Moses' repeated intercession for Israel. Psalm 106:23 says, "Therefore [God] said that He would destroy them, had not Moses His chosen one stood in the breach before Him, to turn away His wrath from destroying them." Amazingly, the Lord heard and responded with redemption to the prayer for mercy. Repeatedly, one person, Moses, stood between divine judgment and Israel's sin, and this one person's steadfast intercession was enough to bring Israel from the place of being oppressed, rebellious slaves to attaining the promises of God and receiving the Promised Land. Let us revel in the power of prayer and the approachable heart of God.

Yet, even as we are awed by the power and mercy released through prayer, some of us, in the subconscious realms of our souls, find another thought forming. At first, it appears as a question. However, because it is often left unattended, for many it turns into a doubt. The problem is this: as we watch the cycle repeat itself again and again— of Israel's sin, of God's threatened wrath, and of Moses' plea for mercy—we are troubled. Is Moses, a mere man, more merciful than God?

The very idea seems blasphemous; we are instantly ashamed that we thought it, so we bury it. Yet, the fact is, for many, the doubt was buried alive and remains alive. For it is true that, had not Moses interceded, the Lord would have destroyed men, women, and children for one short period of sin. Moses does seem to be more merciful than God.

Of course, as good Christians, we dare not voice this doubt; we do not even whisper it to our most trusted friends. As a result, what ought to be a pure and wonderful example of the value and power of prayer, instead, on a more subconscious level, tempts us to mistrust God's goodness, using our doubts to excuse ourselves whenever our goodness fails.

Even if you are not personally struggling with this battle, someone you love probably is or will be. When people fall away from God, often it is because they have sinned and now doubt the Lord's goodness to forgive them.

Thus, we need to clear up this mystery concerning God's wrath. Why isn't God automatically merciful? Why does He warn of judgment, yet reveal Himself in mercy and restraint when even one intercessor pleads on behalf of others?

THE PURPOSE OF GOD

To answer these questions we must return to the first statements the Almighty made in Genesis concerning mankind; we must understand the reason for our existence. Let's read what God Himself declared in the sacred Scriptures as His purpose for mankind. The Lord said,

> "Let Us make man in Our image, according to Our likeness". . . And God created man in His own image, in the image of God He created him; male and female He created them.   —Genesis 1:26–27

The living God has encoded into humanity a grand and irreversible purpose: man has been created to reveal the nature of God. This has been the Lord's purpose from the beginning, and, though the world has continually changed, the Almighty has never deviated from this plan.

We should not assume that the creation of Adam and Eve, however, completed this purpose. Genesis marks a beginning, not a fulfillment. Although Adam and Eve possessed intelligence and freedom of will above that of the animals, God's plan was only initiated in Eden; they were still far from being in the image and likeness of God. Indeed, shortly after they were created, they fell into sin. If they were created in the likeness of God in their essence, how is it that they sinned? Sin is the one thing God cannot do.

Let's think of mankind as a singular person in search of his identity and destiny. For man, Eden is the commencement to a journey that can end only when man attains the image and likeness of God. Man discovers sin, but fulfillment is not there; he receives moral law and tries to obey it, but again, satisfaction eludes him. Having been born in paradise with God, man carries in his primordial soul the memory of paradise lost.

The introduction of Christ into the consciousness of mankind marks the beginning, in divine earnest, of God's action to accomplish His original purpose with man. Christ not only provides payment for man's sins, but also sets the pattern for man's life.

As Christians we heartily agree with the payment of Christ. However, we only remotely accept the pattern He provides. We think the first aspect of our relationship with Christ, our forgiveness, was the goal. It is not. The first purpose is servant to the second. Christ forgives us so that He can transform us.

Man transformed into the image of Christ is the pinnacle truth, the supreme revelation, of God's will for humanity. No truth is more poignantly chronicled by Jesus and the New Testament writers. Every instruction of righteousness points us to the standard of Christ; every apostolic teaching prods us to fulfill Genesis 1:26–27 through the manifestation of Christ within us.

Paul wrote in Romans 8:29 that Christ is the firstborn of many predestined brethren. Galatians 2:20 and 2 Corinthians 13:3 explain that Christ is living in us now, while 2 Corinthians 3:18 assures us that, from the moment Christ entered our spirits, as we behold Him, we each "are being transformed into the same image from glory to glory, just as from the Lord, the Spirit."

We are born again, not just to go to heaven, but to become like Christ. We unite with other Christians, not only for administrative expediency, but also because Christ manifests Himself most perfectly through a many-membered body. We are part of a second Genesis whose goal is to fulfill the first Genesis: man in the image of God.

In scores of Scriptures, some so wonderful their truths will never be fully apprehended on earth, the Holy Spirit repeatedly proclaims the magnificent purposes of God in man. There will be a last trumpet when, with the pains of labor, our mortality will put on immortality (1 Cor 15:51–53), and, beloved, we will be like Him (1 John 3:2)! At that moment, all heaven will celebrate in awe and praise, for "the mystery of God is finished" (Rev 10:7). Man, in perfect submission to God, will bear His glory and power.

Adam never was the prototype. From eternity God's purpose was that man would be conformed to Jesus Christ, not Adam. God chose us in Christ prior to Adam's fall. Indeed, He chose us "before the foundation of the world" (Eph 1:4).

God's purpose from the beginning was to make man in Christ's likeness. When we seek to know God's will, let us seek first to satisfy the call to Christlikeness. Yes, the maturation of this dimension of our lives abides in ascendant purity, far above every other aspect of our existence. Whom we will marry, where we will work, or what church we will attend are important decisions, but they are incomparable to what we become in the attainment of Christlikeness. The reason God created man is so that he would become like Jesus; it is the reason He created you.

LET US MAKE MAN

Yet we haven't fully addressed the relationship between God, man, and the power and purpose of prayer. All we have done is establish that God's goal in creating man was to reveal through him the nature of Christ. Let us, therefore, return to Genesis.

When speaking of the nature of God, the Scriptures proclaim the singularity of the Godhead: "The Lord is our God, the Lord is one!" (Deut 6:4) The Scriptures nearly always refer to God in singular terms. From the beginning, we read that God (singular) created the physical world. But then, when we study His creation of man, we see that the Almighty speaks of Himself in plural terms, saying, "Let Us make man in Our image" (Gen 1:26).

We define the Lord's ability to remain one in nature yet separate in manifestation as the Trinity. One clear example of this paradox is seen in the relationship between Jesus and His Father. Each time Christ prayed to the Father, it was, in truth, God on earth talking with God in heaven. Figuratively, we could say that God separated Himself, became God in two "places," yet remained one with Himself in nature.

Though Jesus Christ bears the likeness of man and represents mankind through the human side of His nature, spiritually He is of the same substance as God. Paul wrote that "although [Christ] existed in the form of God, [He] did not regard equality with God a thing to be grasped, but emptied Himself" (Phil 2:6–7). He was "begotten" (Ps 2:7) of the Father as He entered the realm of time, remaining one with the Father, yet separated organically from the Godhead by human flesh and subjective human experience. As Christians, we accept the mystery of the Trinity even if we cannot fully understand it.

However, this discovery of God's "separated oneness" leads us back to our original question concerning intercessory prayer and why it is able to restrain God's judgments or even cancel them completely. Specifically, what was it about Moses' prayer, the prayer of a solitary individual, that could obtain forgiveness for three million people who had not repented of their sins?

On the surface, Moses seems more merciful than God. But Moses is God's workmanship. Let's look at what God worked into His servant. We can imagine that the highly cultured Egyptians were shocked that Moses, now a mature and popular prince in Egypt, had become increasingly more concerned for the Hebrew slaves. After all, Moses was enjoying the finest conditions that civilization and position in life provided. He had nothing personal to gain, no advantage to be found by identifying himself with Egypt's slaves. Indeed, the Egyptians deemed the Israelites hardly more valuable than cattle. The idea of somehow helping the Hebrews was preposterous. Help them? As a prince in Egypt, Moses owned them!

Yet Moses could not defend himself against the deepening burdens of his own heart. Even against his will, empathy toward the Hebrews was growing within him. From the moment he began to identify with the weaknesses, injustices, and sufferings of his oppressed brothers, the Spirit of Christ set about to awaken him to his destiny. As I said earlier, this act of compassionate identification with those who are scorned, disgraced, or discredited is called the "reproach of Christ," which Moses considered to be "greater riches than the treasures of Egypt" (Heb 11:26).

The process of training, breaking, and reshaping continued in Moses for forty years. Until Christ began His work in him, Moses had been aloof and apathetic toward Israel's need, but with the advancement of Christ into his life, he became God's vehicle to bring and extend mercy to Israel.

Whenever we read of intercessory prayer or redemptive action on the part of one for the needs of many, whether in the Old or New Testament, it is actually Christ manifesting, inspiring, and empowering that individual. Moses bore Christ's reproach and was himself the expression of God's mercy toward Israel.

Therefore, the question of whether Moses was more merciful than God proves to be superfluous. For the spirit of intercession that emerged through Moses was not really Moses' spirit, but Christ's Spirit praying through him on man's behalf. This is significant: man, inspired by Christ, is the primary means through which God brings forth mercy to other men. What we are actually seeing operate through human instrumentality is God in His mercy interceding before God in His justice. At the highest level, intercessory prayer is God talking to God through man.

Remember my earlier statement that God separates Himself from Himself, yet never loses His essential oneness with Himself in the Godhead. When the Lord appears ready to reveal His wrath, He will always, simultaneously, be searching for an individual through whom Christ can emerge in the mercy prayer. The Almighty's primary goal is not to destroy wickedness but to use wickedness in the process of transforming man into the Redeemer's image. If threatening justifiable wrath awakens even one to manifest the mercy of Christ, that one transformed life is more valuable to the Almighty than His need to destroy wickedness.

Without a doubt, God must reveal His righteous judgment concerning sin; otherwise, mercy has no meaning or value. God is revealed in the Godhead as Father, Son, and Holy Spirit. The Father is God manifesting Himself in authority and justice; Christ is God revealed in redemptive mercy; the Holy Spirit is God in manifest power, bringing forth in creative or destructive power the expressed will of the Godhead. The ultimate revelation of God is seen in the unveiling of perfect love; God's wrath is the backdrop. The display of this redemptive love in man is the purpose of man's existence.

Thus, as Christians, our call is to manifest the voice and mercy of Christ to God. In intercessory prayer and mercy-motivated action, we identify with those exiled from heaven because of sin; we unite with those who feel separated from God because of physical suffering, heartache, or persecution. In manifesting the redemptive mercy of God, we embrace the very reason for our existence: to be transformed into Christ's image.

MORE PERFECT THAN PARADISE

God is so committed to man's transformation that He limits much of the administration of mercy so that it can come only through human agencies. Yes, He provides a wonderful variety of life's gifts to all men, and He "sends rain on the righteous and the unrighteous" (Matt 5:45). However, it is human beings who must feed the hungry and clothe the naked; the oppressed will likely remain so until a caring man or woman brings deliverance. The suffering in the world around us compels us either toward hardness of heart or compassion. This is the very nature of life itself: God's mercy enters this world through the narrow channel of the human will.

Thus, the Lord told Moses,

> Behold, the cry of the sons of Israel has come to Me; furthermore, I have seen the oppression with which the Egyptians are oppressing them. Therefore, come now, and I will send you to Pharaoh.
> —Exodus 3:9–10

The Lord says, "I have seen the oppression. . . I will send you." God sees the need, but He reveals His mercy through His servant. So also with us. God sees the oppression and hears the cries of people, but His plan of mercy is to inspire us with Christ, who reaches through us to others. Whether we are speaking of Moses' intercession or the temple offerings of the Jewish priests or the most perfect act of intercession—Christ's incarnation and death—God's mercy finds its greatest manifestation through human instrumentality.

When we hear that the Spirit of God is threatening judgment, the very fact that He warns us gives us the opportunity, even with fear and trembling, to embrace the role of Christ-inspired intercession. God actually desires that we touch His heart with mercy, thus averting wrath. In truth, the primary reason God warns is not so that we can run and hide, but so that we can stand and pray. He seeks to inspire mercy in His people; otherwise, why would He create a world where He allows Himself to be entreated by prayer? Even when the Almighty shows Himself angered, grieved, or poised for judgment, He tells us that He is still seeking a means of mercy. He says, "I [am searching] for a man among them who [will] . . . stand in the gap before Me for the land, that I should not destroy it" (Ezek 22:30).

We can expect that the Lord will thrust us into times of desperation in which genuine calamities or fearful situations loom ahead of us. He warns us so that we can be active participants with Him in the redemptive purpose. And it is in such cases, whether our cry is for our children or church, our city or country, that we are compelled toward God for mercy. For it is often in pure desperation that we grasp and attain the nature of Christ.

To turn and actually call for or demand divine judgment against people is to position ourselves in an attitude that is exactly opposite the heart God desires to reveal in us. Indeed, whenever we judge according to the flesh, there is only one thing we can be guaranteed, according to Jesus. He says, "In the way you judge, you will be judged; and by your standard of measure, it will be measured to you" (Matt 7:2). In fact, God will often stop dealing with the one we are judging and start dealing with us if our attitude is anything but redemptive.

Now, let me state that there will be times when we are called to bring forth God's judgment, but there is a prerequisite. John wrote,

> And we have come to know and have be-
> lieved the love which God has for us. God
> is love, and the one who abides in love
> abides in God, and God abides in him. By
> this, love is perfected with us, that we may
> have confidence in the day of judgment;
> because as He is, so also are we in this
> world.   —1 John 4:16–17

There are times when God brings forth judgment, not in the final sense, but in the immediacy of our world. The word confidence in this context means "free speech." In other words, not until "love is perfected with us" will we be qualified to speak God's wrath. Possessing God's love precedes proclaiming God's judgments. In heaven, we have no authority to judge sin if we are not first willing to die for it.

Adam's failure and subsequent expulsion from Eden seemed the worst of all possible events. Yet from the Almighty's perspective, there were lessons man needed to learn about mercy that could not be taught in Paradise. Indeed, what looks like an imperfect environment to us is actually the perfect place to create man in the likeness of God. Here, we have a realm suitable for producing tested virtue. In this fallen world, character can be proven genuine and worship made pure and truly precious. Yes, it is here where we truly discover the depths of God's love in sending Christ to die for our sins. And here, in the fire of life-and-death realities, is where we become like Him.

Let's pray: *Lord Jesus, Your love, Your sacrifice, is the pattern for my life. How I desire to be like You. I want more than anything to reveal Your mercy, both to the world and to the Father. I surrender all my other rights and privileges that I may possess this glorious gift of conformity to You. I love You, Lord. Use me, pray through me, love through me, until, in all things, I reflect Your image and likeness.*

—FROM THE BOOK, *THE POWER OF ONE CHRISTLIKE LIFE*

SELF TEST, CHAPTER TEN

Remember, we are looking for answers that correspond with this training. Please write out your essay answers, allowing the Holy Spirit to provoke your thoughts. You may want to use them for group discussion. Note: we do not provide answers to essay questions. To check your multiple choice answers, see answer key at end of this session.

Chapter 10, Essay #1: Can you believe that your transformed life is more valuable to the Almighty than His need to destroy wickedness?

Chapter 10, Essay #2: Describe the work of God in your heart as it pertains to this study on prayer.

#1. Yes — my transformed life is God's desire. He wants me transformed.

#2.

1. According to Genesis 1:26–27, what is the Lord's first purpose for mankind?
   a. to live in harmony in the garden forever
   b. to be successful
   c. to create man in the image and likeness of God
   d. to enjoy freedom

2. Christ's first purpose was to provide payment for man's sin; what is His second purpose?
   a. to demonstrate our guilt
   b. to present Himself as the pattern for man's life
   c. to enable us to endure two-hour sermons
   d. to destroy all wickedness

3. What is the "reproach of Christ"?
   a. compassionate identification with those who are scorned, disgraced or discredited
   b. divine judgment
   c. not relating to the pain of others
   d. being kept from associating with the oppressed

4. With the advancement of Christ into us, we become the Father's vehicle to:
   a. condemn sinners
   b. bring an end to worldliness
   c. bring and extend mercy into the world
   d. destroy wickedness

5. What does it mean to say: the highest form of intercessory prayer is God talking to God through man?
   a. we take notes about Jesus' prayer life
   b. this refers only to "praying the Scriptures"
   c. listening to others praying to God
   d. the highest manifestation of intercession is really Christ's Spirit praying through us to the Father on man's behalf

6. Why does it seem as though the Father, in some measure, limits His mercy to work through His people?
   a. God is so committed to our Christlike transformation that He will delay answers until He can reveal His mercy through us
   b. He's run out of available angels
   c. He's very busy running the universe
   d. He's hoping if He ignores us we'll go away

7. Why does the Lord warn of judgment, yet reveal Himself in mercy and restraint when even one intercessor pleads on behalf of others?
   a. because God has mixed feelings about destroying wickedness

b. when one person attains Christlike love and holiness in an evil world, it fulfills the Father's purpose in creating man

c. to embarrass us if we have spoken out about His coming judgment

d. His primary goal is to destroy wickedness; our prayers only delay His wrath

8. When would we be qualified to bring forth God's judgment?
    a. having fasted for 40 days
    b. be asked by a pastor to speak
    c. when Christ's love is perfected in us
    d. being in a leadership position

9. What environment is most perfect for proving our character genuine, our worship pure, and creating us in the likeness of God?
    a. at Christian conferences
    b. in church services
    c. in our living room watching TV
    d. in this fallen world

QUOTE:

"What looks like an imperfect environment to us is actually the perfect place to create man in the likeness of God. Here, we have a realm suitable for producing tested virtue."

ANSWER KEY TO THIS SESSION'S
SELF TEST QUESTIONS:

CHAPTER TEN. God Talking to God
1.c, 2.b, 3.a, 4.c, 5.d, 6.a, 7.b, 8.c, 9.d.

ONLINE RESOURCES FOR

IN CHRIST'S IMAGE TRAINING

ONLINE SCHOOL INFORMATION

ICIT online school was established to empower individuals seeking greater conformity to Christ. Students from around the world register online and then receive two written messages each week via email. They also receive a set of 39 audio teachings (on 24 CDs or cassettes), which complement the written messages and add to the training. Students are then tested every six weeks and receive a cumulative grade at the end of six months; they also receive Level I certification from In Christ's Image Training.

The text materials used by our online school have been upgraded and reproduced into these four Level I manuals. If you are interested in continuing your studies, or if you desire certification through *In Christ's Image Training,* you will need to purchase and study the audio messages that accompany these manuals (see the following resource pages). You will then need to take a separate exam that will confirm to us that you have understood the training materials and are, indeed, pursuing the character of Christ.

For more information about current prices, special offers and the benefits of *In Christ's Image Training,* visit our web site at www.ICITC.org. No one will be refused training due to lack of funds.

LEVEL I BASIC TRAINING
(using Arrow Publications materials)

In Basic Training, the student/group studies at their own pace.

Full course: manuals and audio messages	$172.00
Manuals only (four books: Christlikeness, Humility, Prayer, Unity)	$52.00
Audio only (24 CDs or tapes)	$120.00

Materials available: Four manuals and 39 audio messages
(see back of Unity book for session and audio titles)

*Note: If you purchased this Basic Training package, you can still later enroll in the online school. To officially complete Level I and receive ICIT certification, you must enroll in our online school and successfully pass the final exam, after studying all manuals and audio teachings. Tuition cost for completion of Level I is $68.00. Visit www.ICITC.org for Level II tuition fees.

LEVEL I PREMIUM PACKAGE
(Enrollment in *ICIT* Online School)

When enrolled in ICIT Level I Online School, the commitment is for six months of training via weekly email lessons. Testing will be done every six weeks, following the completion of each track (Christlikeness, Humility, Prayer, Unity).

Individual Tuition	$240.00
Married Couple	$350.00
Group rate (per person, in group of six or more)	$85.00

Materials provided:
Sessions introduced through weekly email
39 audio messages on 24 CDs or tapes (included in tuition)

Benefits of Enrollment in *ICIT* Level I Online School:
Interaction with *ICIT* school and other *ICIT* students
Invitation to annual On-site Impartation Seminar
Certification with *In Christ's Image Training*
Diploma signed by Francis Frangipane
Opportunity to advance to Level II training
Opportunity to advance to Level III training
Opportunity to join Association of Pastors, Leaders, and Intercessors

For more information visit www.ICITC.org.

*NOTE:As an ICIT Level I online student, you are entitled to purchase one set of study manuals at a 50% discount, $26.00, from Arrow Publications.

ICIT MEMBER CHURCHES/ORGANIZATIONS

ICIT member churches/organizations may receive substantial discounts or other benefits for your church or organization when you purchase ICIT materials through Arrow Publications. For the most current offers and news, visit www.ICITC.org.

BOOKS BY FRANCIS FRANGIPANE

CALL FOR QUANTITY DISCOUNTS ON 10+ BOOKS!

IT'S TIME TO END CHURCH SPLITS

Not only is the deception surrounding splits exposed, but we are brought to a place of healing where we can possess the "unoffendable" heart of Jesus Christ.

#FF1-026   retail $10.50   our price $10.00

THE DAYS OF HIS PRESENCE

Published by Kingdom Publishing.
As the day of the Lord draws near, though darkness covers the earth, the outraying of Christ's Presence shall arise and appear upon His people!

#FF2-021   retail $11.00   our price $9.00

THE STRONGHOLD OF GOD

(formerly The Place of Immunity)
Published by Creation House.
A road map into the shelter of the Most High. The atmosphere of thanksgiving, praise, faith and love are places of immunity for God's servant.

#FF2-009   retail $13.00   our price $10.00

THE POWER OF COVENANT PRAYER

(formerly The Divine Antidote)
Published by Creation House.

Takes the reader to a position of victory over witchcraft and curses. A must for those serious about attaining Christlikeness.

#FF2-010   retail $10.00   our price $9.00

THE POWER OF ONE CHRISTLIKE LIFE

Published by Whitaker House.
The prayer of a Christlike intercessor is the most powerful force in the universe, delaying God's wrath until He pours out His mercy.

#FF1-025   retail $11.00   our price $10.00

THE THREE BATTLEGROUNDS

An in-depth view of three arenas of spiritual warfare: the mind, the church and the heavenly places.   #FF1-001   our price $9.00

#FF1-022 **hardcover**   our price $14.75

HOLINESS, TRUTH AND THE PRESENCE OF GOD

A penetrating study of the human heart and how God prepares it for His glory. This classic devotional has become a favorite of teachers, students and all who are seeking to know the fullness of God's heart.

#FF1-002   our price $9.00

THE HOUSE OF THE LORD

Published by Creation House.
Pleads God's case for a Christlike church as the only hope for our cities. It takes a citywide church to win the citywide war.

#FF1-004   retail $10.00   our price $9.00

DISCIPLESHIP TRAINING BOOKLETS
$3.95 EACH (10+ AT 40%, 100+ AT 50% DISCOUNT)

COMPILED/FORMATTED FOR GROUP STUDY BY FRANCIS FRANGIPANE

A TIME TO SEEK GOD   #FF1-020 $3.95

DISCERNING OF SPIRITS BESTSELLER! #FF1-018 $3.95

THE JEZEBEL SPIRIT BESTSELLER! #FF1-019 $3.95

EXPOSING THE ACCUSER OF THE
   BRETHREN BESTSELLER! #FF1-017 $3.95

PREVAILING PRAYER   #FF1-011 $3.95

REPAIRERS OF THE BREACH   #FF1-013 $3.95

DELIVERANCE FROM PMS #DF1-002 $3.95

OVERCOMING FEAR! #DF1-003 $3.95

BY DENISE FRANGIPANE

TAPE ALBUMS
TAPE OF THE MONTH ANNUAL SUBSCRIPTION IS $54.50 (INCLUDING S&H)

TO KNOW GOD   #1FF5-032 4 tapes $20.00

IN HOLY FEAR   #1FF5-036 5 tapes $25.00

PRAYER WARRIOR #1FF5-034 3 tapes $15.00

ON THE ARMS OF OUR BELOVED
   #1FF5-037 5 tapes $25.00

RECOMMENDED READING AND SELECTED CLASSICS

EVANGELISM BY FIRE
   by Reinhard Bonnke   #RB1-001 retail $15.00

INTERCESSORY PRAYER
   by Dutch Sheets   #DS1-001 retail $12.99

THE PROPHETIC MINISTRY
   by Rick Joyner   #RJ1-001 retail $12.99

YES, LORD! (LEARNING COVENANT THROUGH
MARRIAGE) by Sherry Thornton   #ST1-001 retail $12.00

FULL LIFE IN CHRIST (formerly LIKE CHRIST)
   by Andrew Murray   #AM1-001 retail $10.99

WAITING ON GOD
   by Andrew Murray   #AM1-002 retail $6.99

CHANGED INTO HIS LIKENESS
   by Watchman Nee   #WN1-001 retail $6.99

SIT, WALK, STAND
   by Watchman Nee   #WN1-002 retail $4.99

THE GREAT DIVORCE
   by C.S. Lewis   #CSL1-001 retail $9.95

PRACTICE OF THE PRESENCE OF GOD
   by Brother Lawrence   #BL1-001 retail $4.99

CO-PUBLISHED BY ARROW PUBLICATIONS

BREAKING CHRISTIAN CURSES: FINDING
   FREEDOM FROM DESTRUCTIVE PRAYERS
     #DC1-001 retail $15.00

YOU CAN ALL PROPHESY #DC1-002 retail $10.00

THE NEXT 100 YEARS #DC1-003 retail $12.00

BY DENNIS CRAMER

JOURNAL OF THE UNKNOWN PROPHET
   by Wendy Alec   #WA1-001 retail $18.00 our price $16.00

THE BIRTH OF YOUR DESTINY
   by Victoria Boyson   #VBl1-001 retail $12.95 our price $10.95

FALLING TO HEAVEN
   by Mickey Robinson   #MR1-001 retail $12.00

HELP! I'M STUCK WITH THESE PEOPLE FOR
   THE REST OF ETERNITY!   *New!*
   by Susan Gaddis   #SG1-001 retail $12.00